*come
as
you
are*

come
as
you
are

ORVAL H. AUSTIN

 **ABINGDON PRESS**
Nashville • New York

COME AS YOU ARE

Copyright © 1956 by Pierce & Washabaugh

Library of Congress Catalog Card Number: 56-5368

PRINTED AND BOUND AT NASHVILLE,
TENNESSEE, UNITED STATES OF AMERICA

preface

ESPECIALLY in the area around Yellowstone National Park I have seen "Come as you are" on restaurant advertisements. It means: "You don't need to wear formal clothes, nor even coats, to come into this dining room."

Half-shaved, I've answered the telephone to hear a friend say, "Come as you are." It meant: "Drop everything, and come just as you are—you'll find others here in surprised states of unreadiness."

"Come as you are" thus means the ordinary, the average, without pretense or polish. It means excitement aroused by the prospect of looking in upon people unprepared. And thus is derived the title of this little book. It finds reminders of life's deepest qualities in the ordinary events of life. It seeks to capture some of the excitement that comes with the revelation of God's plans and purposes in the commonplace things, when we are least prepared.

These are stories of the exciting ordinary.

When Jesus said, "Come unto me," I wonder if he meant that we should always dress up, put on a long face, silently enter a dimly lit sanctuary dripping with piety. The people who came to him came dripping lake water, smelling of fish, their hands dirty from handling tax money, their skirts rumpled.

Some came on sick beds because others hoped he would heal their withered limbs. Some came with their hopes high. Some came full of devotion because they had been told this Messiah could help them.

5

They came to him and he showed them the birds and the foxes, the widow who had lost her coin, the sower who sowed his seed in unpromising soil. From the commonplace the excitement of God's love was opened to them.

You are invited to come to this book as you are, with your hopes and your fears, your triumphs and your guilts, without pretense. The convictions here are based on the belief that devotion to God should be an everyday affair, and therefore these stories are about things as common as stones and running brooks.

The Bible is central in the conclusions because of my conviction that one must know it, and use it, and trust it, if he is to have ears to hear the Word of God in our day.

To relate the Word of God to all of life is what I believe Paul meant when he said to his followers that they should "pray always without ceasing." And I believe that this must be the attitude with which we go to the cobbler's, the set of mind with which we read the funnies.

Here, then, are many common incidents, first told as a part of a radio series called "A Story to Tell," each of which can lead us to reverence. Here, told in the commonplace events of daily life, is the story of God's help for living in such a world as ours, available to us through our faith in the Lord Jesus Christ.

Come as you are.

ORVAL H. AUSTIN

contents

IV. face to face

V. peace in a world of turmoil

CONTENTS

VI. new start

bored with yourself

Society is now one polish'd horde,
Formed of two mighty tribes, the
Bores and Bored.
—Lord Byron

great day to be half alive

Did you ever wake up and jump out of bed and feel glad that every nerve was alive to face the new day? . . . Ever wake up and wish that you could stay numb for about twenty-four hours?

THERE was the doctor who slammed down his instruments and stalked out of his office—to go see a patient who really needed him. For the fourteenth time that day he'd heard a patient say, "Doc, can't you give me something to ease me? I can't sleep. All this is piled up on me, and I can't take it, and I know I won't sleep. Give me something. . . ."

And there was the mother who got tired of hearing her kids squabble with one another and yell at her; and when they kept on yelling that they wanted to go to the movies, she slammed them into bed, saying, "I'm the one who's going to the movies. I've got to get away. . . ."

This is the Aspirin Age, a great day to be half alive. That's the way we act—as if, "What you dont *feel* won't hurt you."

The world is so full of a number of things, which we don't quite like, that we put off until tomorrow—and then tomorrow —the real facing of our difficulties. It is easier to go numb, with alcohol or sleeping pills—or to run away—than to face the world with our eyes open, our senses alert. Aspirin Age—Great Day to Be Half Alive.

What would you think of a person who came to a doctor and asked for a pair of lenses which would keep him from seeing anything? "Doctor, everyday I have to pass an ugly, filthy hole, that breeds all kinds of disease. . . . Give me a pair of lenses to keep me from seeing it."

We are like the Cheerful Cherub:

> Though troubles help to make us strong
> Every time they come
> We find it hard to think of this
> When we are having some.

I could write a theme song: "Numb me, numb me, till I feel no more." But enough of this irony. The song that is better says: "Feed me till I want no more."

There is a scripture that fits our Aspirin Age like a glove. It is a little-known but beautiful passage in the fifty-first chapter of Isaiah:

Hearken unto me, ye that know righteousness, the people in whose heart is my law; fear ye not the reproach of men, neither be ye afraid of their revilings. For the moth shall eat them up like a garment, and the worm shall eat them like wool: but my righteousness shall be for ever, and my salvation from generation to generation. Awake, awake, put on strength, O arm of the Lord; awake, as in the ancient days, in the generations of old.

"Awake, awake, put on strength, O arm of the Lord. . . ." Christianity becomes a vital force in your life when it meets a deep and consciously felt need. It has no power if you are bored—which is a way of running away.

We are up against destructive forces. If we face our need, and turn to Christ, his faith about life, his way of living life, his power for sustaining life, are food for our hunger, water for our thirst, medicine for our sickness—and power to carry on.

Dear Lord, I am glad to be alive in such a time as this, which cries out for answers. Sustain me in the faith that sees beyond the years to the glorious day when thy kingdom shall come on earth. Work in me and through me to hasten that day. AMEN.

are you bored?

There are chronic bores. Nothing is right with them. Almost anything looks good to them—until they get it.

ARE you like the woman in this little verse?

I wish I had a ticket for Siam.
I'm getting pretty bored with where I am.

Well, let me introduce to you the most bored man in history. His name is Koheleth, which is a Hebrew name. The name is translated *Ecclesiastes* in Latin, and is mistakenly translated "Preacher" in English. On the sly you may admit that preachers sometimes are bores. I won't mind.

But this Koheleth was a king. King over Judea, in Jerusalem, he set out to make himself happy in every way a king could command. But he ended up every time in the same fuddle— bored. He's the fellow who said: "I have seen everything that is done under the sun; and behold, all is vanity and a striving after wind" (Revised Standard Version).

He applied his mind to seek out wisdom, and concluded that it "is an unhappy business that God has given to the sons of men to be busy with" (R.S.V.).

So he tried in turn all sorts of pleasures and wine and houses and vineyards and singers and dancers. And he brags that in all

15

his efforts he became great; and his wisdom did not leave him.

He sounds just like some modern movie star, who gets all that the world can offer, and finds it not enough—and cracks up.

Such is the dread disease boredom, which shows itself in the symptom of Ecclesiastes: "The thing that hath been, it is that which shall be; and that which is done is that which shall be done: and there is no new thing under the sun" (Ecclesiastes 1:9).

Endless repetition maketh the mighty bore.

The rest of the little verse about Siam goes this way:

> But when I'm in Siam why all I'll do
> Is wish I had a ticket for Peru.

Maybe you recognize the symptoms of the disease: You are saddled with the same old routine, the same old problems, the same old bickering, the same old attitudes in people close to you. You grab at something new, and it becomes old and boring. No new thing under the sun.

Well, turn from your Old Testament to your New. There you will find a remedy for the disease.

"Therefore if any man be in Christ, he is a new creature: old things are passed away; behold, all things are become new." (II Corinthians 5:17.)

"All things become new." Does it mean *all* old things are made new? Does it mean the old routine can take on a new look? The old frustration can become a source of pleasure?

It means that. Even pain, and hate, and rejection can be made new. They can become patience, and tolerance, and love.

So, if you are bored, and have been looking for something new to tickle your fancy, look again. Stop your selfish, Koheleth-like demanding. See the wonder of God's gifts. Look to the spirit of Christ. Take him into the old, boring routine. He maketh all things new.

16

I stand humbly in thy presence, my Creator. Thou didst look on all which thou didst make and declare it very good. Make me a creator with thee, as I seek in thy Word for new light on old problems. Help me use my gifts from thee to create a new world for myself and those around me. AMEN.

lost person

Your attention, please!
Have you seen this person? If you find her, you may be able to help her.

I'M looking for a lost woman, a housewife. She has all she once dreamed of having as the things necessary to happiness. But still she's unhappy much of the time.

She has a husband who loves her. She has a fine home, and all the gadgets necessary to make the chores easy. She has enough money to do the things she needs to do, and enough for some of the nonessential pleasant things she wants to do. She has a charming child, who is healthy, smart, and active.

These are the things she dreamed of in those romantic days when she was looking forward. Now she's looking backward, because her days are empty. And she's not an old woman, either. But she's tired. She has achieved a goal, but it does not satisfy her.

Her husband, who once treated her like a queen, now seems to ignore her. And she can't bring herself to try to make him take an interest in her. She resents his absorption in his work. She resents his attention to the child. She nags him, who was once her pride and joy.

The child is a nuisance. Children's clothes get dirty. Children

17

make messes in the kitchen, and in the living room, and in the bedroom and in the bathroom. They ask a lot of silly questions. They scrap with kids their own age. They annoy adults. They tell secrets.

This child, once so affectionately pressed to her young bosom, gets pushed into a corner. Once this lovely child filled her with tenderness. Now, doing the things children ought to do, the child fills her most of the time with loathing.

Her friends, who used to think her witty and gay, now find her as often spiteful, sharp tongued. She thinks they have grown strange. And she criticizes them behind their backs. Sometimes to their faces.

She finds no understanding. She thinks the world is cold and cruel. She's tired, bored, empty.

Have you seen this person? She is lost. I'd like to find her. I have something to say to her. I'd like to tell her: "You are not hopelessly lost. Confused, yes. But not hopelessly lost."

I'd like to offer her the one cure for her condition. No medicine can restore her to her former self, except it be a medicine of the spirit.

I'd like to tell her of a love that passeth understanding. If you see her, tell her this: "Trust in that love will help you to search yourself—and to see that your problem is one of pride. You are selfish. You are thinking of your own interests, and this is wickedness; it feeds resentment. Take the Lord's Prayer to heart, and forgive those about you. They are as deeply hurt as you. Forgive them, for they know not what they do—and you will find forgiveness for your resentment.

"Read the Good Book, and study it so that it can help you. Take such a passage as this from the twenty-second psalm: 'My praise shall be of thee in the great congregation: I will pay my vows before them that fear him. The meek shall eat and be satisfied: they shall praise the Lord that seek him: your heart shall live for ever.' "

Yes. You may help this lost person to find herself, through faith. Take her with you to a church where the Word of God is reverently preached, where something happens to the people who stand and confess their faith together.

"The meek shall eat and be satisfied: they shall praise the Lord that seek him: your heart shall live for ever."

O Thou who breathed the breath of life, breathe on me. I am not half the person I could be. Awaken in me an appreciation of the wonders about me and the hope ahead. AMEN.

a heart set free

Many people, even in countries where freedom is honored, are sick for want of freedom.

A TOWN-BRED girl about eight years of age was driving through the countryside with her parents. She looked out at a farm with a big patch of woods behind the house and a pony looking over the fence, and she said, "I wish I had a pony and lived there—and could do the things I wanted to do."

A simple little statement, but it came from a heart not set free.

She was talking to her father, who remembered his own town-bred boyhood. He remembered how his cousins, who had lived on a farm, with a patch of woods and two ponies, had envied him his freedom in town, and his bicycle.

You cannot have everything your heart may have a fleeting desire for, her father was thinking. He had had a bike and a

19

life in town. And he had longed for a pony and a patch of woods. The cousins had had a patch of woods and ponies, and they had longed for life in town and a bike.

There are some things you cannot do, are not free to do, wherever you are.

In the lonely places you are pestered by a desire to sit down across the table from someone, and talk. You want to go swimming with a gang. You want to go to the movies. A scrap would even be welcome—as an exercise in freedom.

In your so-called free acts you are bound—by instinct, by habit, by self-interest. There is a rebellious spirit, and an anxiety for our very lives which keeps us from being free, until our hearts have been set free.

Among the freest people I have known have been men in prison, where they were confined a large part of every day by cold walls, guarded constantly by men who were never kind, and treated often like dogs—yet they were free. They were free from anxiety for their own lives so that they could plan together with other men for the well-being of all; they could do justice, even mercy, to men who shared their fate. They were free—free to care—because they had found a freedom that did not depend upon the circumstances in which they found themselves.

Not all prisoners are so; but there are some who, by accepting their lot, rise above the circumstances.

And you may find such freedom, to be free in spite of an environment that may now frustrate you.

A Christian, as a new creature, knows freedom in Christ. Jesus was free in his love for the people of the land, in his victory over anxiety for his life.

Through faith in Christ you may be free, able to trust in the faithfulness of God toward his creation. Jesus showed us the way, when he said: "Thy will be done." When he laid down his life having forgiven the malefactors, and commended his spirit to his Father.

"Resist not evil," he said—"resist not the hampering restrictions of living wherever you are; resist not the fact that certain restraints are always around you; but find freedom in love."

Accept the life he has given you. Give your heart freely in love; and you may be able to say: "When I freely gave my love, I found my heart set free."

Why art thou cast down, O my soul? and why art thou disquieted within me? hope in God: for I shall yet praise him, who is the health of my countenance, and my God. AMEN.

how are you?

I guess that's the world's saddest question, because it gets the worst answers —more lies and more unthinking answers. Let's face it—Just how are you?

ONE time I was making a portrait, a photograph, of a beautiful girl. She was about a junior in high school, and rather shy and stiff. It was going to be difficult to catch her beauty and her warmth of personality, unless something broke the ice.

In an attempt to uncover some of the radiance I felt she had, underneath her frozen pose, I said to her, "You look like Dottie Lamour." Which was true. She did look like Dottie, and Dottie was at that time a movie queen at the height of her fame.

But it was the wrong thing to say. It had precisely the wrong effect. The girl was embarrassed, and it took another five minutes, along other lines, to get her to relax and be natural.

I had embarrassed her because she thought I had commented on a wanton streak in her nature, a streak she had felt but had not been able to accept.

She was something she didn't like to be. And she certainly didn't want other people seeing her as she really was.

How are you? Can you accept yourself as you are? Can you wake up and face the day with the feeling that you're glad you're you?

And when you make those inevitable mistakes, can you get along with yourself? Or do you eat your heart out?

How many people accept you just as you are? There are always plenty of people ready to judge and find fault. But we are never really comfortable, or at our best, until we have some people who understand us, accept us, and love us—just as we are.

This is the glory of the Christian faith: God loves us, accepts us, just as we are. Even though you may not altogether like the kind of person you are, God knows, and God cares.

> Just as I am, without one plea,
> But that Thy blood was shed for me,
> And that Thou bidd'st me come to Thee,
>   O Lamb of God, I come, I come!
>
> Just as I am, and waiting not
> To rid my soul of one dark blot,
> To Thee whose blood can cleanse each spot,
>   O Lamb of God, I come, I come!
>
> Just as I am! Thou wilt receive,
> Wilt welcome, pardon, cleanse, relieve;
> Because Thy promise I believe,
>   O Lamb of God, I come, I come!
>
>   AMEN.

why so hot
little sir?

*This is a thing Ralph Waldo Emerson
said to himself when he got too agitated.
Is the prevailing wind in your sails one
of agitation?*

MAILMEN seem to be happy, well-adjusted people, as a rule.
Maybe it's the wonderful exercise in the open air; maybe it's
the people they meet. Anyway, they seem to be a happy tribe.

And we have an especially happy one in our town. He always
has a big smile, even though it's so hot he's wringing wet from
head to toe, or so cold that the rest of the town is buried behind
big collars. Whether it's wet or dry, he always wears a big
smile and has a friendly greeting for everyone.

So it rather surprised me when one day, speaking of
someone on his route, he said, "I wish something would happen
to their dog."

I guess I had thought that anyone who got along so well with
people would naturally get along with all dogs. At any rate, I
was surprised to find that a cross dog bothered him.

So I said, "I'm surprised that a dog like that would cause
you any trouble."

"Well," he answered, "they have to keep it tied up. And
any dog gets mean when you have to keep it tied up."

Who's cross as a bear? Are you? Do you feel mean? Maybe
there is something in you like there is in the mutt—something
which should be free to run and explore, which is tied up.

If your prevailing temper is one of meanness, one of feeling
nasty, it's a warning that something is wrong. There is some
spirit within you that is being frustrated, tied up.

Guess you know what I mean . . . and you'd like to know what to do about it. Well, I know of three things that *help*.

First—and this is good advice for milktoasts—*Get it off your chest*. Surprising how some things seem to dissolve when you face them like a man. You go backing off from problems, trying to crowd down your resentment, or your fear, or your creative instinct; and it turns sour. And you get sour. Face it, and you'll help clean up the mess. The trouble with this approach is that it isn't permanent. You need to go swashbuckling about repeatedly. Something more permanent is needed.

So, second: *Examine the cause for your tied-upness*. It may be that you feel mean because you are selfish. Things don't go just to suit you, so you blow your top. When your wishes may not be the best guide after all! Here is a permanent guide: Examine your frustration. If it is for selfish motives, look for a deeper, wider good. Seek ye first the kingdom of God.

And there is a third thing: We call it *providence*. It means that "all things work together for good to them that love God, to them who are the called according to his purpose."

Take a long look. It's surprising how well things turn out, if love and self-forgetfulness are the tools, even though your momentary wish may be thwarted.

A modern translator says it: "In everything God works with those who love him . . . , to bring about what is good" (Goodspeed). Love of God will unleash your drives and relieve your frustrations.

Great Physician, I seek many things—blindly—even when deep within me I know that what I really need will come only if I seek first thy kingdom. Lead me in the way everlasting. AMEN.

when the going is tough

Welcome, O life! I go to encounter for the millionth time the reality of experience and to forge in the smithy of my soul the uncreated conscience of my race.

—JAMES JOYCE

hard-times label

By'n by hard times comes aknocking at
the door,
Then my old Kentucky home, good
night!
Do hard times mean "good night"?

IF you were going to write your autobiography, you could use
James Thurber's title, *My Life and Hard Times*. No?

Seems as though the end and aim of our effort is to keep hard
times from the door. Still we got 'em. Still we know they're
coming. What to do?

Well, I bring a piece from a fascinating book which might
change your way of thinking about hard times.

Wright Morris, author of *The Inhabitants*, has a little bit
like this: "I can see it coming—a Law, making it illegal for a
man to have a hard time." How do you like that? Sometimes
it seems as if that's what the government's trying to do—keep
everybody on easy street. We are embarrassed when somebody
has a hard time. This shouldn't happen in our land of plenty.
So, pass a law making it illegal for a man to have a hard time.
Put the man off the streets. If you can't put an end to hard
times, at least put them out of sight.

But then, Morris goes on to say (surprise): "If it ain't hard
times makes a man, what is it?"

Now . . . wait a minute. We try to duck all the hardness we
can. And here's a guy who says it's hard times makes a man.

Well, he goes on to say: "If you are going to take the troubles
away from a man—be careful what you take. . . . You may take
away the man instead of the troubles."

And, when you stop to think about it, do you know anybody
who has strong muscles, a magnificent body, who didn't do a

27

lot of hard work and exercise to get that way? And when you come to think about it, what do you have that's really worth while that you didn't acquire the hard way?

Gravy—handed to you on a platter, in bed—never got you anything worth having.

But you take a thing, and put a hard-times label on it, and you either hate it or you think it's something you would love. I know a banker who lost everything in the great depression. Everything except honesty and courage and grit and faith. He borrowed a telephone and promised honest service, and kept a prayer in his heart. And he founded a mighty banking business, while other men ran from a hard-times label.

Are you any different?

I'm not talking through my hat. Hear the Good Book talking: "Woe to them that are at ease in Zion" (Amos 6:1). Amos undoubtedly outraged some fancy people who lay upon beds of ivory and stretched themselves upon couches eating the lambs of the flock, when he told them that by putting far away the evil day they were causing the seat of violence to come near.

And whose is the kingdom of heaven? The first beatitude says: "Blessed are the poor in spirit: for theirs is the kingdom of heaven."

Hard times a-comin'?

Find something worth doing, with a hard-times label on it. Love it. Agonize over it. Give it all you have.

Maker of heaven and earth, Creator of my spirit, forgive my indolence. Forgive my desires for ease when there is so much more I should seek with all my heart. AMEN.

nearsighted musician

Once upon a time there was a poor, unfortunate musician.

YES, once upon a time—and not so long ago either—there was an unfortunate musician. He was nearsighted, and it was difficult for him to read the score when he was playing with an orchestra.

But in spite of the fact that he couldn't see very well, he stuck it out. He played with an orchestra, even though, because of his handicap, it was necessary to memorize every part he played. In order to be more sure of his own part, he also memorized the parts of other members of the orchestra. One day the director became suddenly ill, and the nearsighted musician was recommended as a substitute, because of his knowledge of the music.

When the concert was over, he became the regular conductor of the orchestra. His nearsightedness—his handicap, if you please—had spurred him to higher efforts. And so Arturo Toscanini, probably the world's greatest symphony orchestra conductor, got his great opportunity, partly because he was nearsighted.

Many of the world's great men and women have had handicaps that proved to be blessings. Glenn Cunningham became the world's greatest mile runner after his legs had been so badly burned that it was not probable that he would ever walk again.

"By my God," wrote the psalmist, "have I leaped over a wall." Do you have a wall in front of you that looks like a hard way to go? Maybe it can be a blessing. There are two helps from the Word of God.

First: Adversity has the effect of calling out talents that in prosperous circumstances are never called upon. Paul, Christianity's missionary, had an eye affliction that caused him great pain and impaired his sight. He had some physical weakness that often made him delay his long journeys. He had to endure beatings, punishment, stonings, and exposure. Yet he felt that God had said to him: "My grace is sufficient for thee: for my strength is made perfect in weakness." Rather than forgetting Paul, God was using his suffering to bless him with a greater measure of strength.

To love deeply, to grow strong, to know happiness, we must suffer. It is good to feel that one's life has meaning in God's plan.

The other word from God about facing difficulties is: You are never alone. "Underneath are the everlasting arms." "Yea, though I walk through the valley of the shadow of death, I will fear no evil: for thou art with me."

Do you think that your obstacle is one you can't get over? Then will you take God into it with you? In the blessings of one of the tribes of Israel, Asher, are these words: "Thy shoes shall be iron and brass."

The way may be difficult. If it were all velvet, you could go barefoot. If it were all smooth, like the sands along a beach, you wouldn't need shoes. But where the way is difficult, strength is provided. For hard ways, shoes of iron and brass. "And as thy days, so shall thy strength be."

Forgive me, Father, for complaining of my handicaps, and teach me to use them as steppingstones. AMEN.

life's warning whistles

Soup's on. Come and get it.
How do you know when it's time to eat?

THAT day dawned as any other. And Joe took his lunch bucket and set out for work, as on any other day. He was even a little cautious, because last week he had parked his car in an unusual place at the plant—put it in the shed instead of in the open parking lot—and when the time had come to go home, he hadn't been able to find it. Concluding that he had ridden to work with someone else, he had gone home on the bus and left the car in the shed.

So today he was checking off things as he went. He didn't like the reputation of being "absent-minded," even if he was top research man in the science division.

Joe got to work early, stashed his lunch in the locker, and tackled a problem dealing with some knotty research formula.

The whistle blew—a long blast. Joe took off his apron, washed his hands, got his lunch and ate it. Nobody else was eating lunch, but do you think Joe noticed? He was inclined to be a bit solitary, especially when he had an exciting problem before him.

How was Joe to know that it was nine o'clock? The long blast was a special warning whistle which was set off when the water pressure in certain boilers became too low.

Joe finished his lunch and went back to work. Again a whistle blew. Joe took off his apron, washed his hands, picked up his lunch pail—and went home.

Some of his associates saw him go home when they were going to lunch, but they supposed Joe had arranged to take the afternoon off. The lunch whistle—at 12:00 noon sharp—was Joe's signal for quitting work that day.

How do you know when to eat lunch? Partly habit. Partly the convenience of all concerned. Schools let out, laborers stop, business slows down. There is a community pattern we all agree upon, voluntarily. "This is lunch time," we say.

If solitariness is your way of life, you may eat your lunch at 9:00 and nobody notices. But solitary people miss a lot of the healthy friendliness of life. They are apt to nurse strange wounds and to develop warped ideas. They suffer more than the socially minded people around them.

What a wonderful book is the Bible! Take a quick look at the sixty-eighth psalm. There, in the sixth verse, it says: "God setteth the solitary in families: he bringeth out those which are bound with chains: but the rebellious dwell in a dry land." The fellow who wrote this psalm knew something of the effects of shutting yourself off from people, wrapping yourself too much in your own thoughts. Especially if it is because of rebellion. People who are restrained by other forces are set free; but the people who make *themselves* solitary, because of their rebellion, are apt to get mighty hungry. The rebellious dwell in a dry land. They starve.

Solitary Joe ignored a warning. He got himself kidded because he didn't know a warning whistle from a lunch whistle.

Do you recognize the warnings in your life? You're short of breath, say—too fat. Warning whistle! "You eat too much. You are overeating, in an effort to soothe hurt feelings. Stop." Overeating is a form of rebellion.

You're jumpy and cross? Warning blast! "Better love and forgive more." Accept life as it is; rebel not.

You have a strange pain in your abdomen—food won't digest? Warning! "You strive too intensely. Take time to let God help you."

If you are too solitary to join the family of God in worship, better heed the warnings. Don't get yourself shut off from the friendliness of the Father. He isn't going to kid you about your attitudes. "The rebellious dwell in a dry land."

> O Thou who hast called me friend, make me to know the health and holiness of thy love. When I am tempted to rebel, draw me nearer. AMEN.

the right place at the right time

Did you ever think how important time and place are in life? Maybe you've missed a train—or an appointment with the beauty operator?

THE boy came off the floor with a sheepish look at the coach, and sat down on the end of the bench. Three personal fouls in three minutes.

His substitute was cold, and in about three more minutes the coach called the kid and said to him, "Now get in there. And remember—don't stand around flat-footed. Find a hole and make for it."

Seemed as though the kid just couldn't stay out of trouble. In practice sessions he looked good. He could shoot clean and handle the ball. But when he got in competition, he was always getting tangled up with other players. Forty times that season the coach had drilled it into him: "You're valuable to us only if you can shoot. Keep moving. Get into an open space—right place at the right time."

Life is a game. Some people play it with pressure tactics, like the general who won his battle by getting there "the fustest with the mostest." Maybe you can ride down the opposition, win your way by sheer force of will.

For some, it's skill at dodging the blows life deals that makes them victorious. Maybe you can weave like a good boxer, and manage to "duck" most of life's difficulties.

For most of us, however, life is like a basketball game. Sometimes we get fouled up, running into people. Sometimes we lose the ball. If we can keep our heads in the struggle, we can find a hole: a place where we are needed, where we may be in a position to receive a pass—and get it away again to where it will do some good, before we are fouled up.

It is strange, what a powerful influence for good one little kind act can be. Often it comes at a time when it makes all the difference in the world. Like the simple act of a professor's sharing his umbrella with a homesick boy, which I read of the other day. The boy was far gone with homesickness, walking with his coat collar turned up, across a wet campus, lonely and discouraged. He heard a friendly voice say, "Walk with me, lad," as the prof extended his umbrella. Instantly the clouds vanished, and the boy was happy and hopeful once more, glad to be in college. Through all the years since then, the prof's umbrella has seemed to be above him. And now he says, "To walk with him through college years was to walk with him forever."

Your good acts, in the right place at the right time, can have a powerful effect. The prof was the kind who was always finding a hole and stepping into it.

All around you are people who need a helping hand, a kind word. Jesus, our Guide, was always finding such a hole and stepping into it—feeding the multitudes, healing the lepers, giving sight to the blind, praying for the forgiveness of those who knew not what they did.

Have you walked with him? To walk with him once is to

walk with him forever. He will step into the hole in your life, and will help you fill the gap in the lives of others.

"Inasmuch as ye have done it unto one of the least of these my brethren, ye have done it unto me." A cup of cold water to the thirsty, a visit to those who are sick and those in prison. . . .

Do what you can to help, for love of God and of your neighbor. You'll be in the right place at the right time.

Dear Lord, it's so easy to become confused in the game of life. Remind me often of my place in the scheme of things, as thy child, thy hands and feet and lips, to serve in the little things that present themselves close at hand. AMEN.

my friends

Magic words, aren't they—"My friends"? They have captured the imagination of many voters. Words that turn your isolation into companionship.

THERE was a man who had many friends. But he never had many at one time! And they didn't remain his friends very long! And they never loved him very much, while they were counted among his friends.

Something was wrong with the way he treated them. Something was out of kilter in what he expected of them.

He *thought* he was doing right, because he thought he was basing his attitudes on the Bible (which just goes to show you how careful you have to be when you use it).

He had read a passage that goes like this: "Ye are my friends, if ye do whatsoever I command you" (John 15:14). And he had figured to himself, "If you read it in the Bible, it's bound

35

to be true. . . . Therefore, friends are people who do what you command them!" And he tried to treat his acquaintances accordingly. He would command them—until they got tired of it and of him. And then they wouldn't come when he called.

Let's look at this passage a little. If this is true, in the way in which the man tried to apply it, then a slave master is the best friend. And Hitler had more friends than anybody, during his rise to power; because he had more people following his commandments!

Then, was Christ wrong when he said, "Ye are my friends, if ye do whatsoever I command you"? Or was the man wrong when he thought he could apply it to himself and could command people and expect them to be his friends? Was Christ making dictators? Was he himself a dictator?

Maybe you have seen the flaw in the man's reasoning. You are Christ's friends, if you do what *Christ* commands you. And this is just at the opposite pole from the selfish, demanding, slave-master approach the man was applying.

But it's still true, and it still applies to friendship in general. You'll be Christ's friend, and you'll have true friendships with those around you, if you follow his commands.

How about your friendships? Do you have lots of true friends, who would do anything in the world for you?

There is a mighty difference between doing anything in the world for a friend because you love him, and doing things for a person because he commands you.

Our world isn't as good a place for making friends as it once was. We're on the move too much, too much wrapped up in our own little worlds. Too few of us love unselfishly, are willing to give up our lives for our friends.

Everyone is still hungry for friendship, and if you don't have your share of it, it's because you haven't followed Christ's commands sufficiently. He said to abide in him, to love him and continue in his love, to love one another as he loved you. And "greater love hath no man than this, that a man lay down his life for his friends."

If you are isolated and unfriendly, here are a diagnosis and a remedy all at once for your condition: Be a friend—as Christ was a friend. Think not of what you can get, but of what you can give.

No relationship in the world will work right—boss to employee, parent to child, wife to husband—if the basis is one of demanding. No relationship in the world will go wrong if Christ's commands are followed.

Father, I'm not satisfied with what I did yesterday. Too many times I was selfish and thoughtless. Help me this day to be a true friend wherever I find myself. AMEN.

the way you build a fire

We live in an engineering age. Everything's finely calculated to do a job. And some people are beginning to wonder if the atomic age may do its destructive job too well. What is efficiency?

TWO men had their offices side by side. And both offices were heated by open fireplaces. The older man would come in an hour or so before he began to work and build a fire. When he was ready to settle down, the office was cozy.

The younger man tried to do likewise. He would come in, build a fire, and leave to return in an hour or so. But when he came back, he had only a flicker of flame in his grate.

37

For a few days the older man, seeing the situation, would fix up the fire while the younger man was away, so that it would begin to warm the office. And finally, he said to the younger one, "Who ever taught you to build a fire, anyway?"

"Well," said the young man rather shamefacedly, "I guess no one ever did. Why?"

Said the other, "If you won't think it rude of me, I'd like to explain the principles of fire building so that you can warm your office without taking half a day to do it. If I insult your intelligence, please forgive me.

"First you take some kindling, and put it on some loosely crumpled paper in the grate, like this. One stick won't burn well by itself. So pile the wood up, so that it touches in some places. But be sure to allow enough air spaces so that the fire can get oxygen.

"Then, after the kindling has caught well, place coal on top, in the same way—pieces touching, that is (because one chunk of coal won't burn by itself). But allow plenty of air spaces between the chunks. Then pile the coal up. Heat rises. Fire burns upward. After you get a good fire going in the middle, it will be hot enough to spread to the coal outside."

The young man appeared grateful, although the older man might have insulted his intelligence. And since then he has been able to get his office warm in fairly short order.

If I insult your intelligence, and you've been building fires for years, let's consider a little application. Did you ever think, in your fire building, that society is like a fire?

One person by himself doesn't spark much. He's apt to stew around with his own troubles, and to rehash old memories. And he stays pretty cold.

Let two people with the same interests get together, and ideas are apt to leap and glow.

Get enough people together, and you may get mob violence.

A necktie party in a western movie is the result of the heat that develops when you get enough people together—without enough air spaces between. It takes air spaces so that everyone in the group has room to breathe, or someone gets smothered.

Religious fervor has been likened to a flame, lighted by the Light of the world. Religiously, one person by himself gets pretty dull. But if you want light and warmth, don't hide your light under a bushel. Add more fuel to it by sharing it with others.

The persons who get warmth and comfort from their faith (don't you know it?) are the ones who are mixing regularly with others who share the same light. They keep air spaces—maintain their individuality—but the group is better for it.

Therefore Paul says: "Neglect not the gift that is in thee, which was given thee by prophecy, with the laying on of the hands of the presbytery." (I Timothy 4:14.)

Help me, my Father, to think together with others in the spirit of living and giving, to demonstrate the warmth that can be ours when we get together for a noble, single purpose. AMEN.

faith looks up

I recognize
Power passing mine, immeasurable,
God.
—ROBERT BROWNING

devotional digestion

Do you feel that good digestion is a blessing? Or do you believe that your attitudes have something to do with the way you digest your food?

LET us look in on the breakfast of a friend of mine. This morning, as every morning, he gets down his devotional books and prepares what he calls "devotions" while his wife squeezes the oranges and scrambles the eggs.

He reads a passage of scripture. Dutifully. Then he looks in another Bible, a different translation, and he reads the same passage in that version. And he compares it with a third translation. And if there is any doubt about the passage (some of the words may be different), he turns to a commentary, a recent one which lists all the purest texts, and he learns why certain words have been changed or omitted.

Then he says a prayer, asking God's blessing, and wonders while he eats if he'll be able to digest his breakfast; or whether the many tiring difficulties he'll find at the office will spoil his digestion.

It's a wonder—the way some people come so close to real help from God's Word, and miss it. My friend comes close. He's dutiful and habitual. But it's like trying to wash his hands with rubber gloves on.

My friend reads the passage in John's Gospel which goes: "I am come that they might have life, and that they might have it more abundantly." And he discovers that the word "more" is not in the oldest, the purest, manuscripts. So the passage is found in the modern versions this way: "I came that they may have life, and have it abundantly." And my friend spends his devotional period wondering about the difference between having life abundantly and having it more abundantly. And then he wonders if he'll have a sour stomach.

While all the time there is life abundant, including good digestion . . . provided that he first digest the scripture. Devotional digestion is the best guarantee of good biological digestion.

"I came," says the Good Physician, "that they may have life." Not that they may debate the scriptures. Life, not haggling.

There is help for living in God's Word. But it doesn't do much good to have the Bible lying on the table in the guest room. Nor does the help spring out at you because you read it from a sense of duty. Nor does it help to use the Book as a guide in debating.

"Seek, and ye shall find," it says. Read it to discover its great truths. Study it to find its application to your own life at this very moment. Read a passage and ponder it until the meaning God has for you—*just* you—becomes crystal clear. Believe it. Remember it. Carry it through the day. Let the spiritual principles Christ pleaded for guide your life. Take a look at your problems, or your inner conflicts, and then open God's Word and read until you find a promise that will speak directly to these problems.

But don't treat it like an exercise in debating.

Thy spirit is good; lead me in the land of uprightness. Quicken me, O Lord, for thy name's sake: for thy righteousness' sake bring my soul out of trouble. AMEN.

glowworm faith

Is your faith like the old song about the little glowworm—"glimmer, glimmer"? Does it give a little faint gleam now and then, when the night is black?

A CHILD asked his father, "Daddy, what's a glowworm?"

And his daddy said, "A glowworm is an insect, something like a firefly, which makes a light in the dark."

And with all the simplicity of a six-year-old, the child said, "Oh." The subject was apparently settled.

And very shortly thereafter the child received a watch, a toy, with a radiant dial. When the youngster learned that it would glow in the dark, he tore for a closet and shut himself in. There came from the closet muffled sounds of delight, which indicated that the child was overjoyed at having something that gave off light in the dark.

When he came out, he asked, "Daddy, is this a glowworm?"

The father thought back to the conversation, when the child had appeared to understand his definition of a glowworm, and realized that the child had not understood as much as he had seemed to.

But that is a very understandable confusion, because I know some grown people who don't know the difference between their faith and a glowworm, or a radiant dial.

Is your faith a glowworm? Something that gives a faint glimmer now and then when the world is blackest?

Is it a toy radiant dial, which you carry into the blackest closet, just to see if it glows?

I know a man who committed adultery on the strange excuse that he wanted to see if he still loved his wife! And I also

45

know some people who are doing things they know are wrong, apparently to see if they still love God! They are like the youngster going into the dark closet with his radiant dial. He didn't want to see what time it was—just if it glowed. These people aren't interested in what faith will do for them—just, "Is it there?"

Is yours a glowworm faith, one which will faintly appear if the darkness all around is black enough? I guess everyone, when he comes to his wit's end and is completely beaten, relies at last upon faith. And I suspect that some of the black moods you have, dark depressions, are really self-pity. You get to feeling as though you are at the end of the rope—to discover a faint glimmer of faith.

Faith should glow. The "glimmer" of the glowworm song is too weak. Faith should shine with an intense heat, like the glowing of a bed of coals when a fire has come to its hottest point. We talk about the brightness or warmth of a color as "glowing." We speak about intense excitement of emotion—a mother "glows" when she first holds her new baby.

Faith should *glow*. Christ said: "I am the light of the world." His light drives out the darkness of superstition and doubt and sin.

Get close enough to him to catch some of his intensity, when he said, "Not my will, but thine, be done." Feel the warmth of his love when he said, "The glory which thou gavest me I have given them; that they may be one, even as we are one." Glow in the reflected ardor of his words: "Ye are the light of the world. . . . Let your light so shine before men, that they may see your good works, and glorify your Father which is in heaven."

Sense the depth of his love, the earnestness of his purpose; and you won't have glowworm faith. You will be the light of the world.

Let me live for one purpose, O Christ, to love thee, so that I am willing to live only for thee, to die for thee if need be. So shall my darkness become light. AMEN.

humility

Today's good word . . .

THERE was once a musician. As a young composer he pleased the public ear. He prospered, and was praised on every hand for his music, his fine horses, his beautiful wife.

But he passed off the praise. "Bah, it is nothing," he would say when someone tried to praise him. "I do as I *must*. It is not important if they like it."

And as time passed, his music became too intense, too magnificent, for the simple villagers. They no longer understood his creations; and they began to criticize him. They urged him to create simpler things, which they could understand, to meet the public demand. But he could not. His income fell off. He lost his fine horses, his lovely home. The day came when his wife pawned her wedding ring to buy bread.

To the well-meaning folk who urged him to write the kind of music they would buy, he said, "This I cannot do. I write what I hear; and this I cannot touch."

They called him proud, realizing that he was humble with regard to everything but his music. When it came to his music, he was a lion; because, he said, "This is a gift of God."

He was not proud. He was living as God had shown him he must. He was humble, as Martin Luther was humble. Jesus once said: "Why callest thou me good? there is none good but one, that is, God." He was humble, claiming nothing for himself, But when it came to his relationship with his Father, he was a

47

Lion. Did he not say: "Heaven and earth shall pass away, but my words shall not pass away"? (Matthew 24:35.)

Humility is the surest sign of strength. The humble man is the man who knows what God has given him to do—and does it without fretting, without thought of self, without caring what others think, without fear of failure. He knows the will of God and does it.

"For whosoever exalteth himself shall be abased; and he that humbleth himself shall be exalted." (Luke 14:11.)

As a housewife and mother you may be exalted—by exercising the gift of loving and caring which God has given you. As a businessman you may be exalted, by humbling yourself to do the will of God—and giving more for the money received than men require of you.

Are you seeking peace and strength? Humble yourself. Be the person you actually are before God. Take whatever there is in the world that helps you to find God, and leave the rest aside.

O Lord, whose favor is life and in whose presence there is fullness of peace and joy, grant such an abiding sense of thy presence that it may help me rise above the cares of this world and know that all things here shall work together for good. AMEN.

faith looks up

There are some downcast people.
There are some things that cause us to look down. Some to look up.

ON a summer's day when the distant hills were blue, a barefoot boy bounced along a country road. Dust lay an inch deep in the wheel tracks. Head in the clouds, dust slithering with every step over and between his toes, the boy was alive to every beauty around him.

Then the feel of something different beneath the dust flashed a message to his brain. He scraped his toes in the dust, and uncovered a gold watch chain. His instinct told him that it was a good chain, valuable. He fingered it with excitement, and finally pocketed it—after transferring a pound of assorted items from one pocket to the other so that the chain would have a place all its own.

So starved was he for things of value that he resolved to tell no one of his find, but to keep his treasure a pure secret.

And as he went on down the road, he no longer bounced. He dragged his feet. If he could find a gold chain in the dust, what might not lie buried there? His eyes, which had been flitting previously from hills to thrush to apple tree, were glued now to the dust.

What he missed, he'll never know. He kept his eyes down, looking for treasures that might lie in the dust.

Many people keep their eyes down, looking for treasures in the dust. And if this boy had continued to find treasures by keeping his eyes down, he might have formed a habit of looking in the dust. It happens to some people: they find so many treasures-of-earth that they fail to look up, and thereby they miss a greater treasure.

This boy was treated more kindly by providence. His chain lost its charm; and he learned, before the habit was too deep, that the real treasures of earth lie not in the dust. Nowhere on earth. He learned that a song can be more valuable than gold. He is no poorer without the chain, which has long since disappeared; but his life would be a poor thing, indeed, if he had not this song in his heart:

My faith looks up to Thee,
Thou Lamb of Calvary,
   Saviour divine!
Now hear me while I pray,
Take all my guilt away,
O let me from this day
   Be wholly Thine!

May Thy rich grace impart
Strength to my fainting heart,
   My zeal inspire;
As Thou hast died for me,
O may my love to Thee
Pure, warm, and changeless be,
   A living fire!
       AMEN.

know where to look

There is something to be found, if you know where to look.

A SEVEN-YEAR-OLD, in a bit of a peeve because she couldn't do exactly as she wanted to at the moment, came shouting into the kitchen, "Is Mommy here?"

Her daddy, not liking her tantrum, looked slowly all around the kitchen, so that the child would get his point: If she had simply looked, she would have known that her mother was not there.

But the child wanted words. So she demanded, "Is Mommy here?"

50

"Well, let's see," said her daddy, suiting action to the words, "maybe she's under this plate." Then he moved a chair and said, "No, sir, she's not under this chair."

The girl stamped off angrily to find her mommy. And she learned the lesson in one application. The next time she came looking for someone in obviously the wrong place, she, said, "Oh, never mind. . . . I'll find her."

Which is a simple story to illustrate a simple point. Knowing where to look is important.

The simpler your wants, the more places there are to look. I can stand on a corner on the village square, for instance, and see at least twenty-two places where I can buy chewing gum. When my wants become more complex, the places where I may find them answered are less common. For instance, there are fewer places where I can buy a pair of socks. And if I want to borrow a hundred dollars, or build a house, or get a television set repaired, I have to know just where to look.

How about your complex wants? Do you know where to go when you are possessed by a vague anxiety and want to find peace of mind? Or when you are unutterably lonely? Or when you are burdened by a sense of guilt? Do you know where to go?

It's a good thing to stop once in a while and recognize the fact that we are often looking in the wrong places. We feel lonely, so we believe the ads and run out and buy a lot of merchandise that's advertised as if it were the only thing needed to gain popularity. We don't like to face the fact that we are fearful, insecure; so we run to shows and parties, pretending that we are all solid. Trying to find Mommy under a teacup.

For your most complex needs, the answer is in the Word of God. You may get help from complexion soap, if you are lonely —some help. But the final answer is, "Lo, I am with you alway."

Fearful, insecure? Sleeping pills may seem to help for a time.

But know where to look, and you'll get the answer: "Be of good cheer; I have overcome the world."

Guilty? A thief may get temporary relief from stealing something. But in the Word of God you learn that there is real forgiveness—to be found in forgiving your brother and loving him, and in seeking the Lord while he may be found.

There is simple, satisfying help for your complex, torturing needs. Know where to look.

Dear Father, do with me as thou wilt, put me where thou wilt, deal with me freely every day. Only show me the way. AMEN.

tightrope faith

The strength of a rope depends upon how you use it. And how about your faith?

ONCE upon a time there was a boy who weighed about eighty pounds. It was forty pounds adventure and forty pounds imagination. In his explorations he came upon a piece of rope, a small rope but long enough to stretch between the two trees in front of his house. He saw himself, naturally, as a tightrope performer.

But first (he had learned some things from the school of hard knocks) he went to his father (who knew everything) and asked him, "Daddy, is this rope strong enough to hold me?"

His daddy tested the rope and said, "I think it will hold you, son. . . . It'd probably hold a horse."

The youngster stretched the rope as tightly as he could between the trees, about six feet above the ground. Full of confidence, because Dad had said it would hold, he started at one end to walk the rope. After about three steps the rope broke, and he came down in a heap.

He ran crying to his father, whom he accused of double-crossing him. But his daddy said: "You didn't say how you were going to use the rope. It would have held you if the weight had been hanging down on the rope. It would take a much stronger rope, stretched horizontally this way, to hold you."

Once upon a time there was an adult who launched out on a great adventure. Was it the establishment of a marriage? Was it the rearing of a child? Was it a new business you set up?

Before the adventure you checked your faith: "Father, will my faith hold?" The answer was, "Yes, my child, your faith will carry you."

And then something broke. The marriage hit rocky places. The child was ungrateful. The business lost money. And what happened to your faith?

"Well, my child, how did you use your faith? Was it leading up, straight up, to a strong support? Or did you try to stretch it along the world?"

A thin thread of faith will hold, and will see you through rocky places, and ingratitude, and dishonesty—if it stretches up.

Are you looking for something that will carry you through the cares of the day, something to overcome the ingratitude of those around you, or their indifference? Are you looking for something that will carry your weight and the weight of your problems?

"For verily I say unto you, If ye have faith as a grain of mustard seed, ye shall say unto this mountain, Remove hence to yonder place; and it shall remove; and nothing shall be impossible unto you." (Matthew 17:20.)

Verily I say to you, a thin thread of faith, which leads up

53

to God, will support you, in spite of everyday evils, though they appear as big as mountains.

> I will lift up mine eyes unto the hills, from whence cometh my help. . . . Thou art my light and my salvation. . . . Thou art the strength of my life; of whom shall I be afraid? AMEN.

how to grow rich

What is the combination that opens the door to good fortune? Is there a trick?

OLD Granny Smith—we'll call her—faced the tax assessor. He looked around her plain little living room as if he were looking for something he couldn't find.

Granny tried to be helpful. She said, "Oh, yes, that new rocking chair—my boys got together and gave me that for Christmas. They couldn't rightly afford it, and I can't rightly enjoy it, it bein' so fancy. . . . But you will want to count that. I don't have any idea what it's worth."

The assessor still looked unsatisfied. "You sure you ain't got some hidden assets somewhere?"

"Well," she answered, "I guess I have $32.00 in the bank."

And then his reason for being unsatisfied came out: "But I've been hearin' that you was a rich woman."

"Oh, that," she said. "I've heard that too. And I do have riches. But not the kind you can write up in tax books. I wouldn't be any good without my riches, but they wouldn't be much good to you for raisin' money on."

He didn't know quite what she meant. He said so.

"Well, I have friends. I guess those are about the greatest riches a body can have. I have a fine family, and they love me. I have faith, which sees me through hard times and which gives me a reason to be thankful, and to share my joys. These are my riches. I guess they are what you'd call 'treasures in heaven.'"

We're all searching for riches, I guess. How to get recognition for our talents, or how to acquire the house in the country we've been longing for all our lives. Or how to meet the girl of our dreams. Or how to start a new business.

And the answer to all these things is the same. Behind every story of success is a story of faith. Without the oil of faith to light the lamp, none of the great dreams of men could have been realized.

One trouble with most of us is that we have always associated faith with the supernatural, something for Sunday which has nothing to do with Monday. But faith is something that can give us riches every moment of the time in the everyday affairs of our lives.

The farmer sows his seed, and you watch him reaping the harvest; and you think there is nothing strange in this familiar procedure. You see the scientist at work in his laboratory, and you know that sooner or later his experiment may succeed. *This* may be the year that conquers cancer.

Because you cannot see faith, you may doubt that it is a strong power, creating the only riches. But it is the greatest force in the world.

At every hand the universe is yours, ready to fill your every need. Yet you may be reluctant to trust the same law by which the seed is brought to harvest. You may doubt that that same power would stoop to concern itself with you.

"If ye have faith as a grain of mustard seed, ye shall say unto this mountain, Remove hence to yonder place; and it shall remove; and nothing shall be impossible unto you." (Matthew 17:20.)

Granny was right. If she had faith, she was rich. This same treasure in heaven may be yours, if you will take what God has created so abundantly.

Hear my prayer, O God, and consider my desires. Give me a quiet spirit, a loving, friendly, and useful manner of life that may be devoted to thee with my whole heart. AMEN.

trivia

There are places where three roads meet. And thereby hangs a tale.

THERE is a kind of crossroads talk, the kind of talk that goes on when people meet casually. The kind of talk that goes on today in villages when people meet at post offices to pick up their mail. The kind of talk that used to go on when they met on the depot platform to watch the 4:10 come in.

What do they talk about? The weather . . . how many shirts you have in the laundry . . . Junior's earache . . . the latest news about the young girl who threw herself at the handsome stranger. . . . Small talk.

Well, go back in civilization a couple thousand years, to Roman days. People met; and people gossiped. They talked about the weather. They talked about how many togas there were in the laundry. They talked about the good old days and the bad young neighbors. Small talk . . . the same kind of small talk.

And where did the Romans meet when they were giving us the roots of our language? They met not at railroad stations or post offices. They met at the crossroads. I know, because it is written into our language.

The conjunction of three roads was an important place. People who had few gadgets and little diversion met there to swap notes with their neighbors and passers-by. A Roman came home with some small talk about a neighbor. Asked where he had heard it, he said, "Down at the three-way." He came in with some unverified information about Caesar's latest battle. Where had he heard it? "Down at the three-way."

The Roman word for three was "*tri*." The Roman word for way was "*via*." He had heard it down at the *tri-via*. The place gave its name to the kind of talk that went on there. And now when we say that something is unimportant, trifling, we say it is *trivial*.

But now that I've told the story behind the word, I wonder if anything is really trivial, in the sense in which we use the word. I wonder if anything is unimportant.

Since small talk persists, and people have been swapping the same kind of notes for thousands of years, I believe it is important. In spite of the great world-shaking changes, in spite of dictators, and science, and philosophy, people are interested in people.

Sharing is important. Feeling as though you belong is important, and probably as important as any other single thing in our world. And small talk is a common denominator, the thing that draws us together.

Scorn not your neighbor's interest in her petunias, or in her backache. There is someone to whom nothing else is so important at this very moment as the rash on a baby.

A nuclear physicist cannot talk to many people about the anatomy of the atom. But he can draw close to a composer, or a bricklayer, or an executive, if they have children who are cutting teeth at the time.

Simple folk talk about simple things, and this is important. Because it draws them together, creates a bond. It dissipates some of the loneliness of living. If you want to make a brother out of a stranger, share his interests. The wonder of the atom is no greater than the wonder of the click of a first tooth against a spoon. All things are important.

Paul says: "All things are yours. . . . And ye are Christ's; and Christ is God's." (I Corinthians 3:21, 23.)

Almighty God, whose mercies are without number, whose treasures are infinite, I give thee thanks for all the gifts thou hast bestowed on me. Help me to see the worth of every one. And draw me closer. AMEN.

queer money

Counterfeit is known to the trade as "queer money." You may not know much about it . . . but there are many kinds of counterfeit.

I ONCE knew a counterfeiter who had been sentenced to a federal penitentiary for counterfeiting half dollars—while he was an inmate of a state prison.

That's right. While he was an inmate in a cell in a state prison, he made counterfeit half dollars. He had a friend in the auto-mechanics school who brought him bearing metal. Another inmate friend brought him casting plaster from the dental office. He had a hot plate in his cell, because he made coffee there for a certain shift.

He'd make a mold from a half dollar, melt up some metal, and cast a bunch of queer dollars. Then he'd crumble up the mold and get rid of the evidence. Of course, some guards had to be in on the deal. They passed the queer money in town and brought back cigarettes and candy and stuff to the prisoner.

He didn't get much for his queer-money activity—except a year in "Uncle Sam's Big House."

That's one of the things about counterfeit—you don't get much for your money. It doesn't take much real money to buy a whole slew of counterfeit money, if you know where to get it. It's true also in the spiritual realm, where there's a lot of queer money. If you can't get the real coin of the realm, you pile up a lot of counterfeit.

I know some people who can't get the real coin of the realm of the spirit which we know as love. And so they take a counterfeit substitute. Lacking the real thing, love, they look for thrills. They look for mastery. Or they count their conquests with the opposite sex. All counterfeit. It takes piles of the substitute to equal a little bit of the real thing.

Some people know they miss the real coin of the realm, happiness. So they pile up huge amounts of self-praise. Or they try to buy friendship by having big cars and big dinners.

They tell me a lot of fat people are fat for the same reason. They are hungry for understanding, or for acceptance, or for love. But they are unsatisfied. They find some relief in eating. They eat and are not satisfied. Queer money, in the realm of the spirit. Queer as a three-dollar bill.

How well do you know your Bible? Do you know that the phrase, "They shall eat, but not be satisfied," comes from the Good Book?

How well do you know yourself? Do you know when you are enjoying real coin of the spiritual realm, and when you are trying to satisfy your needs with counterfeit?

If you are on a wild-goose chase, trying to show your acquaintances what a wonderful person you are, to satisfy your deep need for approval, you are trading in counterfeit. Or if, in your search for love, you are always having to prove your lovableness, you are not getting the *real* thing.

You need to go back to the source where you can find out about the real coin of the realm. Forget yourself. Love others without demanding anything in return. Love God, seeking first his Kingdom and his righteousness, and you'll find satisfaction. You'll be able to say, "My cup runneth over."

Most of my experiences are satisfying and genuine, O Lord, because I am thy child. Help me to know what makes things go wrong, when they do; and teach me how to deal with false things. AMEN.

face to face

Resignation gently slopes the
way;
And, all his prospects brightening to
the last,
His heaven commences ere the
world be past.
—OLIVER GOLDSMITH

face to face

One of the toughest, meanest characters you ever met . . .

I WANT you to meet my friend Jacob. He doesn't have any last name—just Jacob. But he doesn't need any more names to identify him. Once you get to know him, you'll never forget him, because he's so much like yourself.

Jacob was the kind of character who would have got himself shot for a cattle rustler in the days of the Wild West—always thinking of himself. Willing to steal anything for himself, he fooled his dad and cheated his brother, Esau, out of the family spread, by pretending that he was a rancher and making himself smell like a herdsman when the old father was on his deathbed.

Mean, he was—and scared, too. He ran away from home when Esau got up a posse and started after him. But he must have had a good streak in him, too, because on his way to his uncle's ranch while he was running away from his brother, Jacob dreamed a dream about a ladder up to heaven. And God was in that place. . . . Most villains have a conscience.

"And Jacob awaked out of his sleep," the story goes, "and he was afraid. . . . And Jacob vowed a vow, saying, If God will be with me, and will keep me in this way that I go, and will give me bread to eat, and raiment to put on, so that I come again to my father's house in peace; then shall the Lord be my God."

Well, now! Jacob didn't want much, did he? Just for God to give him his own way, look after him, supplying all his needs and babying him in everything he wanted. Then, great big boy that he was, he'd *allow* the Lord to be his God!

Well, Jacob went on his way. And he went to live with his uncle, Laban. Laban cheated Jacob out of seven years' labor

63

before Jacob could get the daughter he wanted for his wife. But Jacob was a persistent cuss, and he worked.

But for seven years he schemed how he could get even with his cheating uncle. And Jacob was not a good man to trifle with. I suspect that if Laban had known his stripe, he'd have given Jacob the wife he wanted and sent him on his way at the first. Because after a while Jacob, in good old villain's fashion, had managed to get the most and the best of his uncle's beef herd for his own. The scheme looked legitimate enough while it was going on, but it made Laban mad when he found out about it.

So Jacob had to run away again. His uncle was about to string him up. And Jacob takes his family and his herd and runs. He starts for his old home country. And he is now, as they say, between the devil and the deep. Esau may be waiting for him just across the border. But he's got to run or Laban will catch him.

Now Jacob really gets religion. He really faces God for the first time. He prays another prayer. This time he is humble. This time he doesn't say, "If you will bless me in the way I go. . . ." He says, "I am not worthy of the least of all the mercies, and of all the truth, which thou hast shewed unto they servant. . . ."

You have witnessed the conversion of a vicious man. From one who wants to have only his own selfish way blessed by the Lord, to one who is humble, recognizing he has received more from God than he deserves—this is a long, long way.

And after his conversion, Jacob saw God face to face.

Friend, how about you? Are you trying to tell God how to run your life? to suit your selfish ways? Is Jacob's first way your way? Then you are wondering where you can find peace of mind and happiness.

And when you come to Jacob's second way, the way of humility and of seeking, by God's grace you may find the peace of mind and happiness you seek.

Thy right hand be exalted, O Lord. Help me to live for thee, to do thy will, to be a grateful, humble seeker, that I may declare thy works—that I shall not die but live. AMEN.

a low estate

Blue mood . . . end of the rope.
What do you do when you hit rock bottom?

LET'S suppose, just suppose, that you are a new inmate at the Federal Penitentiary at Terre Haute. You've been dragged through the courts; you've lain for months in jail. You've been utterly humiliated.

And you've had a long time to ponder your estate in life. What seemed like a harmless sort of thing, at which you got caught, has become in your mind a very loathsome thing. You are guilty, and you torture yourself with wonder about why you did such a foolish thing.

And now, in a poor frame of mind, you have reached the end of the road—a prison. You have been photographed, fingerprinted, examined by the doctors. And now you come into the dining room for your first meal.

You follow the line of men into a tremendous room, with long polished wooden tables, and a row of steam tables across the far end. It is—even in your state of mind you can see—an attractive room, with its smooth limestone walls and row of high windows.

While you are waiting for the line to move, you notice a row of letters carved in the stone walls, just below the high windows. It's an inscription. Your eyes naturally fall first on the letters across the front of the room. You read them, and a shock goes through you, for the letters read: *Thou art reduced to a low estate.*

You wonder what kind of torture chamber this is going to be. You know you're low. You've pondered your wrong for many long hours. But do they have to hit you in the face with it? At every meal will you have to look at that thing and see this brutal reminder: "Thou art reduced to a low estate"?

The line moves. You get your beans and stew on a tray and follow the line to a place at one of the shiny tables. You can't keep your eyes from the inscription. And gradually you come to realize that this is part of a bigger inscription, which reads in full: *Take what is brought upon thee cheerfully when thou art reduced to a low estate: for gold is tried in the fire and acceptable men in the furnace of adversity.*

A thrill goes through you. Maybe this isn't a torture chamber after all. Maybe this thing, which you don't understand fully at once, is intended to inspire hope in such low-estate people as yourself. Gold is tried in the fire and acceptable men in the furnace of adversity. Maybe, just maybe, this prison term can be a trial in adversity, through which you can find your usefulness.

What to do when you are at a low estate? Unless you trust in the Word of God, it may be small comfort; but in the Word of God you do find that men are tried in adversity. In the words of Isaiah, the Lord speaks to his people:

> Behold, I have refined you, but not like silver;
> I have tried you in the furnace of affliction.

If you trust the Word of God, there is no depth that cannot be turned to good purposes. All things then work together for good.

O Lord our Lord, how excellent is thy name in all the earth! who hast set thy glory above the heavens. Help me to see that beyond the trial is justice, and that to him who perseveres is the crown. Speak to me and lift me, that I may serve thee. AMEN.

across the street from everything

Fine advertisement for a hotel: "Stay with us. . . . You will be located just across the street from everything."

IT WAS my eight-year-old daughter, Nancy, who said it. We were walking home from the store—that is, I was walking and she was skipping and hopping on one foot, up and down, all around me, in the tireless energy of eight. And she said: "I wish I lived just across the street from everything."

And I suspect that you, as I did, wonder just what she meant. Well, her "everything" included the Empire State Building and Radio City and Jones Beach. We had just returned from a visit to New York. The Empire State Building had been a topic of conversation for weeks; and when we got to New York, we went atop the building and looked out over the city. And we had dreamed and hoped to see Jones Beach and Radio City. And she had got there. High points in the life of an eight-year-old.

So her everything was made up of high points, the novel and the exciting. She didn't think of her doll, which she loves; or of her school lunchroom, or the radio she listens to while she's recovering from an illness. Nothing humdrum in the "everything" she'd like to live across the street from.

67

How's your eight-year-old streak? Wouldn't you like to live across the street from high points—nothing humdrum or stale? Simply to be able to walk across the street to something new and important and exciting?

It's the way of the world.

Nancy forgets that once her doll was "everything" to her. And she can't visualize how boring it would be to climb the Empire State Building the fortieth time.

At eight Nancy hasn't considered the impossibility of doing everything, even if it were just across the street. The world is so full of a number of things that even if you could get them just across the street, time wouldn't permit you to see or do more than a tiny fraction. A day at Jones Beach would cut out a day doing something else, even so. Life would still demand choices; and—just stop to think of it—how many things you'd get that you wouldn't like!!

But most important, Nancy doesn't realize that she *does* live just across the street from everything. In a sense, it's true. In many senses it's true, in this free land of ours. Just across the street lies unlimited opportunity. But sometimes it is a hard street to cross.

As simply as we can cross a street, we can find novel and exciting high points. There's a world of books and magazines and radio and television that brings everything within reach. If we're too busy or too bored or too rebellious to appreciate and enjoy them—well, we have a street to cross.

Across a street, a street called "neighborly love," lies a land where everyone respects and understands you. It's a hard street to cross.

Across a street called "God's will" lies the enjoyment of all experiences that come your way. Learn to accept what comes as bearing a revelation of God's will, and everything you see will be a high point.

Open mine eyes, Lord. Help me to see the greatness of the opportunity that lies before me. Guide me with thy counsel, and afterward receive me to thy glory. AMEN.

honest abe steen

Would you think you could learn something from a counterfeiter? Not me— I'm no counterfeiter. I mean, could you learn something from the story of a counterfeiter?

HALF of what I know has been learned from crooks or thieves or counterfeiters. I mean, it was impressed upon me by crooks. You see, for almost five years I was a chaplain in one of Uncle Sam's big penitentiaries.

And I believe that you can learn something from thieves, and con men, and thugs and hoods and counterfeiters.

As for instance, now, this counterfeiter whom I'm going to call arbitrarily "Honest Abe Steen." Ironical, you think, to call a character who makes imitation money after Honest Abe?

Well, it wasn't because he was honest, although he was an excellent craftsman. He could have held the top job of engraver with any outfit. He knew the trade.

But they called him Honest Abe because he was so fond of the Great Liberator. He was so fond of Abe Lincoln that he did portraits of him all the time. Had a sort of mania for it. And he put Lincoln's picture on all his bills, not only on the five-dollar bill where Uncle Sam puts it. On his ones and tens and twenties he put Honest Abe. And that, you might guess, was the reason for his downfall. A G-man called one day and wanted to look around at Abe's place, because he had tied up the "wrong" dough with the character who was so much interested in Honest Abe. And so they nabbed him.

Do you like that story? Did you learn anything from it? And I don't mean simply to put Lincoln only on your five-dollar notes. . . .

I mean something more like this: Perhaps Abraham Lincoln was such a power for good that even when someone tried to use him for evil ends, the good triumphed in the end. Give it a western-movie-style moral.

But that is close to what I want to say. You cannot fool about the deep and vital things of life. You can fake some things. And you can get by, faking, for the time being—maybe even prosper. But playing false has a flaw in it every time. Like using the wrong picture on the paper money. You cannot fool about the deep and vital things.

Do you know anyone who can fool you with his laugh? Can you pretend to think that something is uproariously funny, and fool the person who knows you best—say your spouse?

Can you fool anyone with your piety, your honesty, or your depth of conviction? Can you take a firm stand for something you don't believe in—and keep up your pretense for long?

All right . . . suppose for a while you can fool people about your depth, or your piety, or your honesty, or your love. Can you fool yourself? Can you fool God?

You can't fool about the deep and vital things. Hypocrisy marks you, and finally breaks you. My best friend among the doctors agrees with me that if people were to live honestly, expressing their true convictions, showing forth exactly what they love, standing firm for the things they believe in—down deep—the number of cases in his office would be cut in half.

Honest Abe would say: "Don't deal from the bottom of the deck." Paul says: "Though I speak with the tongues of men and of angels, and have not charity, I am become as sounding brass, or a tinkling cymbal."

Frankly I like Paul's example better than Honest Abe Steen's. "As sounding brass or a tinkling cymbal." . . . Could you think of any description of yourself as a human being you'd like less?

But I've got a warm spot in my heart for Honest Abe the counterfeiter. He gave us a story that shows the necessity of dedicating one's life honestly to the Highest.

Dear Father, I want to follow thee in everything I do, to be honest and forthright as I must to follow thee. Faith will move mountains. Help me to remain true to this faith. AMEN.

the great allergy

Well, how's your allergy today? Got hives from eating some food you can't tolerate? Nose runny? Aches in the joints? Is your allergy showing?

THE room was full of conversational people, all chatting, having a wonderful time. One of the young women suddenly burst into the flow of talk with an arresting, "Why look at my thumb! It's all red, and throbbing."

Sure enough, the thumb was red, angry looking, and swollen.

Various guesses were offered about what might be the matter with the thumb. Perhaps she had been bitten by some kind of spider, or insect. No . . . no bites.

The thumb consumed the attention of the woman who owned it. She would break into the conversation frequently with references to her thumb, like: "I was just sitting here and

71

found myself rubbing it with my finger—like this. It was uncomfortable, I guess."

Then one of the other young women offered this explanation: "Maybe you're allergic"—she gave a knowing glance at a bouquet on a coffee table—"to *magnolia* leaves. I find . . . (sniff) . . . that they affect me."

When the swelling began to appear in the fingers adjacent to the throbbing thumb, the owner decided that it was time for them to go home and pay the expensive baby sitter.

The discovery of allergies has provided a great source of conversation (or maybe I should say, "conversation stoppers").

I'm not saying that if the woman had gone home when she first thought about the cost of baby sitting, she'd never have developed the swollen thumb. But I do know that there is a Great Allergy in our world, responsible for a lot of spiritual sniffles, which we could do something about. We are allergic about being forced to take a stand.

I know a doctor who rarely takes a stand. This doctor listens until the patient says what *he* thinks is wrong—and then agrees with him. I know a professor who lets the students in his classes guess about his opinion on any subject. He will not declare himself. I know a salesman who won't tell the customer which color looks best on him. Every color the customer tries on is, somehow, "just the right color for you." I know a club president who never knows what his club will do.

Sniveling, don't you think? But are you prepared to take a stand? I know some good church members who don't stand up for their beliefs. They may object to what goes on around them, but they're afraid they might be unpopular if they stood out against it. And there is little difference between these people and those outside the Christian fold.

They'd have a lot less spiritual sniffles if they'd take a stand. Can you say with Paul: "I am not ashamed: for I know whom

I have believed"? Paul faced life's worst—shipwreck, stoning, imprisonment—without sniffles.

And he said: "Whosoever believeth on him shall not be ashamed."

It may take some thinking to know what you do believe. It may take some courage to say, "We also believe, and therefore speak."

But if you'd parade your faith—know what you believe and take a stand for it, and for him—your life could be as free of sniffles as Paul's. And you might do as much good in your way for Christ's cause.

I know whom I have believed. Give me the courage of my convictions. Give me the grace to speak bravely of that faith of which I am not ashamed. AMEN.

an empty jug

You've heard that an empty barrel makes the most noise. . . . Well, this is about an empty jug.

TWO men stopped at a roadside stand where pottery was displayed, and each bought a jug. This wasn't along a modern highway, near some widely advertised tourist attraction. This little scene took place in old Roman times, before the time of Christ. Even back then, before men had learned to speak English, and Latin was their native tongue, they made and sold pottery along the highway.

And then, also, some of the makers of pottery were inclined to fool the public. Because although one man's jug was a fine bargain and he used it many years, the other man's jug didn't last very long. It had had a crack in it, which soon showed up; and the jug had to be thrown away after a short time because it wouldn't hold water.

This empty jug that wouldn't hold water made a tremendous noise, because it gave us one of the strongest words in the English language; and we still acknowledge the cracked jug when we use this word.

Go back to Rome for a minute. And to the pottery stall by Roman road. There were cheats and shysters who made a regular practice of hiding the cracks in jugs by filling them with wax (which was called "cera" in the Latin tongue).

And it became widespread practice, so obnoxious to the reputable dealers in jugs that these honest men put signs up above their merchandise saying, "without wax." They wanted their customers to know that they sold dependable jugs, which were as good as they appeared to be. In Latin the words that meant "without wax" were "sine," without; and "cera," wax. The two words were "sine-cera."

This, then, is the story behind the word "sincere." To be sincere is to be without pretense, to be as good as you pretend to be.

And this is a mighty important thing to be. Do you see why the empty jug made a big noise? I believe the most important personal attribute is sincerity. I know that the surest way to lose your friends is to pretend to be something you are not. And the best way to lose your health, your money, and your happiness is to go around with a false front, trying to appear to be something you are not.

You are looking for happiness? Look where there is sincerity. Be honest yourself. You have lost the zest that makes for the enjoyment of living? Someone has been insincere—maybe it's you.

Do you know that this is the one thing Jesus condemned—insincerity? He blasted a fig tree that promised to have figs on it but was empty. And this is a parable of the old, insincere, empty religion of the Pharisees.

"Woe unto you," he said.

Alas for you, you hypocritical scribes and Pharisees, for you lock the doors of the Kingdom of Heaven in men's faces, for you will neither go in yourselves nor let those enter who are trying to do so. . . . You blind guides! straining out the gnat, and yet swallowing the camel! . . . You clean the outside of the cup and the dish, but inside they are full of greed and self-indulgence.

All the teaching of history, all the wisdom of your own heart, all the wisdom of Jesus—all say the same thing: To be sincere is an absolute *must* in life.

Blessed is the man who has found some honest belief in which he can put all his heart, all his life—an honest faith that affords complete outlet to all the forces that are within him.

Lord, I believe. I believe that thou art the Truth. I believe that the Truth will set me free. Help thou mine unbelief. AMEN.

the funnies aren't funny

So you open your favorite funny paper —and there, any day, you find at least one hero clobbered.

WILL this detective character come to in time to catch the mob? Are they going to keep on piling grief on the hero? How long will the girl reporter suffer before she "wises up" to her rival and justice triumphs?

These are "funny-paper" questions. But they don't seem a bit preposterous in our day, when our news columns are filled with worse things. Don't we have enough of excitement, unending crises, bloodshed, and tensions, without having violence and defeat spoiling the favorite reading of millions, the "funnies"?

Back in my college days—in that boom period that followed the War to Make the World Safe for Democracy—I knew a girl who felt that she was living two hundred years after her time. She romanced about the Paris of the Three Musketeers. She longed to live in the smoky cellars of French Revolution days, when there was brewing a ferment of freedom. Men and women lived dangerously. They threw away their lives gladly—for a cause. At least, they did in the novels which she read.

"Ah," she used a sigh, "those were the days."

Today there is another kind of ferment at work. Youth of today are more apt to say, "Those *will be* the days"—when we can fly dangerously to Mars and Venus, and there throw away our lives for the great cause of conquering outer space.

She, the pre-Depression college girl, wanted to escape from meaningless boredom. The youth of today want to escape from meaningless confusion. They think that the frontier is gone. And if we could just conquer new worlds, we wouldn't be so anxious about the tensions and injustices of this one.

We read the funnies, where heroes win and suffer and win again, because they help us to forget the hopelessness of our world. In the funnies the heroes always win. The villains always die. We want to escape from a world where taxes go higher to pile up more bombs. We want to escape from a world where men can kidnap a child, collect ransom money, and then shoot the child. So we daily follow the exciting fortunes of funny-paper people who, we know, are bound to come out right.

Blessed escape. Blessed, short-lived, disappointing escape.

Times are never right. My pre-Depression friend thrilled over the inspired people who stormed the Bastille and set France free. Yet the very people she read about in novels were the people who refused to escape the injustices of their day. They were surrounded by people who lapped up the stories of the ancient heroes of Greece, to escape the contemporary frenzy. There must have been bored, and scared, and unimportant people who lived close to the cellars where the Revolution was born, wanting no part of the cost of freedom.

The times when Jesus lived were hard times. Rome held the people from which he came in practical slavery. And the words of the scared people about him have not lived. These people escaped; and for their escape they went to the gladiators' games where men fought to the death.

The words which have lived from those dangerous times are the words of men who accepted the challenge of the times—and gave their lives that meaning could be found in the chaos.

The adventures of a funny-paper hero are not worth remembering. Escape is not the way. You can live dangerously and like it, if you can see the danger as a stimulus, and not as a hopeless imposition. This is a good time to be alive—if you can get the feeling that you are part of something important and lasting.

Father, who art ever near, I thank thee for the memory of all who have braved hard times and the loss of all things except their faith in thee. Give me courage in darkness and hope to wait for better days. AMEN.

he came to himself

How far is it to the kingdom of God?

I WANT to tell you a story about a boy, a farm boy who got tired of living on the farm, tired of listening to Papa's advice all the time, and took off on his own. Like all children, apparently, who develop a great thrust for independence along about high-school age, he began to feel a need to develop a sense of his own importance. He rebelled against family restraints. So he said to his daddy, "Give me the share of the property that will come to me."

His daddy, recognizing the youth's need to grow up, split up the profit from the farm and gave the son his share. And the son, in his blindness, went off to a far land, and there spent his money and his life in the wildest extravagance.

His money gone, when famine was stalking the land so that everyone was hungry and bread lines were forming to take care of the needs of honest workmen, he finally landed a job feeding a farmer's pigs. And he got so hungry that he would have stuffed himself on the food that the pigs ate. But nobody gave him anything to eat.

Then, the story goes, he came to his senses. He began to realize that he was not made by God to waste his life in foolish rebellion, just in order to be independent. He began to realize that the "playboy" approach to life was not enough. He came to himself. He realized that he was a fool to go on hurting himself just in order to get away from his family's restraints. Because, at least, he would have enough to eat at home. Independence, he learned, demands that the independent one carry some responsibility.

So he decided to go home and say to his father, "Father, I have done wrong in the sight of heaven and in your eyes. Please take me on as one of your hired men." And what did his daddy do? He put a fine robe on him and made a great feast for him. For the son he had thought was lost was alive. "And they began to get the festivities going."

Now this is a story about happiness, a parable of the kingdom of heaven. Jesus told this story, which you may find in the fifteenth chapter of Luke, to say that every person (though he may rebel from the way that God made him so that he should live most happily) may find his way to the kingdom of heaven.

How far is it to the kingdom of heaven? . . . This story tells you. It is as far as it was from the boy's first request to his last one. For first he said, "Give me . . . that which is mine." And at last he said, "Take me back." From "give me" to "take me." That's how far it is to the kingdom of heaven.

This isn't a remote story about a farmer's boy in a far country in a distant age. This is your story and mine. If you are looking for lasting happiness, you will not find it by demanding what is yours, and going out against the world to find happiness by insisting upon your independence. You've tried that. . . . We all do.

But when we come to our senses, we realize that the true basis for lasting happiness is dependence upon God. You can't storm the gates to the kingdom of heaven. These gates are won by coming to the realization that you don't deserve to be called the child of God—and you don't have rights to take what is yours and go off with no thought of others.

Looking for lasting happiness? Come to your senses. Say to God, "Take me." And you will find that the Father is welcoming you back with great rejoicing. This is the Way.

Father, take me. AMEN.

low-grade infection

How's your health today? Are you feeling right pert? Maybe you're feeling a little below par. Need a pick-up?

ONCE upon a time there was a man. He was a big strong man—looked the picture of health. He'd had a bout with influenza which had hung on for a long time, but he had apparently made a complete recovery. Strong, ruddy complexioned, he was.

Then, suddenly, something hit him. He felt weak, got pale. For no apparent reason. Had a little temperature, but none of the other symptoms of anything that might make him sick.

After a day or two in bed he was his usual buoyant self. But, in about three weeks, he did it again. Got weak and pale, perspired easily, ran a little temperature. After a couple of days in bed he felt all right.

And in about three weeks it happened again. Same signs; no severe symptoms; he just didn't feel good. This time he called the doctor.

The doc took his temperature and his blood pressure, thumped his chest, listened to his heart and lungs, took some specimens. Finally he said, "Come down to the office. We'll take a picture."

Then the diagnosis: "You've got a low-grade infection, secondary to the influenza you had several weeks ago."

The man didn't know whether to be insulted or not—to think that anything he might have would be low grade. But he was relieved to find that he didn't have a really insidious disease. And after six months of spending twelve hours out of twenty-four in bed, with proper food, he was as good as new.

Do you have a low-grade faith? Because, come to think of it, faith is like an infection. As bacteria enter into the body, and there grow and develop and change the whole function of the body, so faith enters into the spirit, there to grow and develop. . . . And it alters the whole life.

And faith can be contagious, too—spread from one to another.

It's possible to have a low-grade faith: one that partly changes the life, hangs on without having any effect, most of the time, occasionally to break forth in a symptom of remorse, or one of a desire to do good, or even a flash of joy. But it soon subsides, leaving the victim looking *apparently* his normal, complacent self.

This is the sort of life led by the person who thinks it would be a good thing to have the strength and the joy that truly religious people have—but can't quite leave behind the desires for things of the world, the love of self. Low-grade faith.

Real health of the spirit comes from really being consumed —wholly infected—by a high-grade germ of faith, by a faith germ that won't be discouraged by halfhearted feelings.

That's the kind of faith David had when he wrote, "The Lord is my shepherd. . . . He restoreth my soul. . . . My cup runneth over."

How full is your cup of life? If you want it to be full, if you want to be able to say, "Surely goodness and mercy shall follow me all the days of my life . . . ," let this high-grade faith consume you.

Dear God, too often my life is empty, although I strive to do my best. I am full of pride and power one day, and of depression and hollowness the next. Help me to live a full and healthy life. AMEN.

peace in a world of turmoil

> And thou shalt find
> Strength when life's surges rudest roll,
> Light when thou else wert blind!
> —JOHANN CHRISTOPH FRIEDRICH VON SCHILLER

day of
the big noise

*Any grain of sand is big to a watch.
And any noise is big if it's right in your
ear. Little noises, if they are close enough,
can drown out big thoughts.*

I WENT to a certain barber shop for the first time. The barber had some noisy clippers, and the barber liked to talk. Not an unusual combination in such places. But somehow this barber had failed to learn that conversations must be timed.

He put the clippers up behind my ear, against my skull. Then he tried to talk to me. My head was filled with clipper noise, so naturally I asked, "What did you say?"

He repeated whatever it was that he had said. And I answered him. Then he put the clippers up against the bone again, filling my head with buzzing, and tried to talk to me. He spoke loudly this time, loudly enough to be heard above the noise. And I answered him above the noise.

Then he was through with the clippers. All was quiet. And he yelled at me, "Do you think we have a chance to win the game tonight?"

He had come to the conclusion that I was practically deaf. It took me some time to explain, and he felt rather sheepish when he did understand, that I could hear him easily enough in a conversational tone if only he didn't fill my head with noise when he was trying to talk to me.

This is the Day of the Big Noise. The world is a barber shop. Everyone is getting trimmed; and the buzzing noises shut out the finer sounds that might be heard.

You know what I mean. There is so much buzzing noise about Communists in government that we can't rightly appreciate our democracy. There is so much rattling going on about divorce rates that we can't appreciate the thousands of couples who live wholesome and happy lives.

There is a lot of interference. We are like TV sets too far from the sending station—the picture and the sound alike are drowned out in a lot of snow and static noise. It's a law of life that you may hear life's finer sounds only if you are tuned to them, and if they are not destroyed by big noise.

Long ago it was said: "Be still, and know that I am God." If it were necessary then to be still, in those quiet days, how much more do we need to be quiet now!

But I have great faith—faith that we are not deaf, only deafened. There are still guiding, comforting, strengthening voices to be heard—not in the earthquake, nor in the wind storm, nor in the buzzing clippers of life.

There is a voice that can be heard through the noise, a voice that says, "You are a child of God . . . of infinite worth." I know. . . . I've heard it. There is a voice that says, "Take time to be holy." I know. . . . I've heard it.

How can you shut out the clamor of the world? Well, there are no deafening noises in the house of God. There is the whisper of an organ. There is the sound of God's Word. There is a prayer for guidance, a voice of hope.

You may bring turmoil with you into the house of God, or the noise of selfishness. If you do, be sure you'll miss the finer sounds that might be heard.

But if you will become able to shut out the noise and strife while in the house of God, it will be easier to cope with the world's Day of the Big Noise in the privacy of your own home, in the silent watches of the night.

Seek ye the Lord while he may be found.

Lord, sometimes I am discouraged, and sometimes I'm lonely, and sometimes I'm threatened by the noise of the world. Take me in thine arms and shield me. I shall find a solace there. AMEN.

somebody kick me

Ever feel like a good swift kick would do you some good?

THERE was a boy who in his college days took a job to help pay expenses. He spent most of one winter building an apartment in a spacious attic that belonged to an uncle of his. Before the job was done, he got himself in the middle of a touchy situation.

His uncle's oldest daughter ran away from home. And she had confided more in the boy than in anyone else, had spent hours up in the attic while he nailed on wallboard. He knew where she had run away to. And she trusted him.

When the boy went to the house, after she had run away and shared her secret with him, he found difficulty in facing his uncle; for he was directly in the uncomfortable middle. The uncle talked about her, and the boy was honor bound to keep still. Later the boy would see the girl, and she'd talk about her father.

It was hard. Too hard for the boy in his green college days. He quit going to the attic—actually left the job undone. Years later he still feels ashamed to think of it.

But the worst part of it was that the uncle never did bawl him out, never asked him when he was going to finish the job he had started. The uncle seemed to sense the delicate position the boy was in, and spared him the necessity of explanation.

The uncle would greet the boy as usual when they happened to meet.

But he never bawled the boy out. And the boy carried the guilty feeling, for having not faced the situation, for a long, long time. If the uncle had just once called the boy a nasty name, or told him off, or given him some kind of punishment, the youth could have faced the situation and got the job done. Punishment is sometimes a very necessary thing. It cleanses, at times when we realize our mistakes and feel guilty.

There are, of course, times when punishment is of no value —and is actually detrimental. When the punished person does not recognize his guilt, for instance. Spanking when the child doesn't know he has done wrong does no good—for the child. But when he has done wrong, and feels estranged from his parents because he's done an unworthy thing, the right punishment will clear the air, and right feelings can be restored. Punishment can be a cleansing, restoring thing.

This is a truth mankind has always known, and many means have been used to punish the body to cleanse the soul. Some so-called holy men lie on beds of spikes. There are some sects today whose members whip themselves. The Hebrews spoke often about the wrath of God.

But our Christian faith gives us a truer revelation of our loving heavenly Father. He sent his Son to bear our shame and guilt for us. He is the Sorrowing Servant, acquainted with grief. He bore our shame, in order that we, by believing on him, may be cleansed of our guilt—and finish the jobs we start.

If you have a guilty secret, and feel as if you need a good swift kick, repent and believe on him.

Dear God, we all fail. I have fallen short, leaving undone jobs that I have started. Help me find the peace and strength, through faith, to forge ahead, leaving the dead past behind. AMEN.

the wicked flee

Here is a story from our own day which demonstrates some of the truths of the Good Book.

A YOUNG car thief rolled along in a stolen car, relishing his success. This was a smooth job, and he had a smooth car. Only the best was good enough to tempt him to steal. And he'd done it again. Clean getaway. No telltale evidence. Time enough before it would be discovered for him to get clear across seven states. He'd taken care of all the evidence. Paint changed. License changed. Numbers fixed. Accessories added. Papers in order. No chance for discovery. He was getting good! This could go on for a long time.

He rolled along easily—no need for speed. Speed might attract a cop. Take it easy. Get out of this state and then think about selling the car. Stay within the speed limit. No questions asked.

Then he became aware of a car following him closely. He watched it, forgot it; he looked up—it was still there. He looked again. State police—trailing him. Were they suspicious? He slowed down. The coppers slowed down. He stepped up. They stepped up. Stayed right with him. What did they know? No!! They couldn't know anything. They couldn't suspect anything. He tried to relax, keep an even pace.

He came to a stop sign—a through highway. And he thought fast: These coppers are following me. Maybe they got some goods on me. If I stop, they'll start asking me questions. I need to get some distance. I'll sneak in here between some of these cars . . . busy road. I'll get on the highway and lose 'em.

So he ran the stop light. Took a chance on the traffic and got in a line the cops couldn't possibly break—and opened her up.

Two miles down the road they pulled him out of the wreck.

The cops looked him over, and one said, "Son, what made you run that stop light? We wouldn't have paid any attention to you if you had obeyed the law. Now we got to book you." They booked him—and discovered the crime.

What made him run the stop light?

Here's where the Good Book talks: "The wicked flee when no man pursueth." How do you like that? The author of Proverbs *couldn't* have known anything about car thieves and their consciences and running stop lights. But he did know something about human nature. "The wicked flee when no man pursueth."

Well . . . chances are you are not a car thief. But the same truth applies to ordinary wickedness just as well.

Did you ever tell a lie to someone and then find yourself getting nasty toward that person? Coming to hate him as though he might have been the one who lied to you? Fleeing, when no man pursueth? Afraid he might discover your lie? Afraid to let him get too close?

Or that little secret nastiness you've been harboring, thinking you were getting away with it. It makes you do some foolish things. The wicked flee when no man pursueth. Isn't that the truth?

And, thank God, it shows the way to take as well as the way to avoid—for the rest of the verse is: "The righteous are bold as a lion."

Dear Master, come and reign in my heart. Dispel the uncertainty and double-mindedness within me, and make me faithful to thy call. AMEN.

the rule
of thumb

Wouldn't life be easy if there were a few simple rules, which you could understand and follow, which would take the confusion out of life?

THE doctor listened to the man's request. "I want a regimen," the man said. "Give me a simple sheet with a schedule for taking certain things at certain times, and I'm sure I can control these attacks."

The doctor glanced at the sheet that contained the man's medical history. It showed a long history of nervous indigestion. All the known remedies had been tried at one time or another.

The patient's history was one of constant tension. Every time he was forced to take a stand, make a decision, run the danger of someone's contradicting him, he became extremely tense. He'd face a difficult decision, and his face would turn white. He'd try to figure some way out without having to be positive. Then, after the ordeal was over and a decision was arrived at, he'd go limp. Nothing would digest.

So now he wanted a regimen—a rule of thumb. He wanted the doctor to prescribe a pill to be taken at nine o'clock, a glass of milk at eleven o'clock, a simple meal of soup and crackers at twelve-thirty, an hour's rest after lunch . . . that sort of thing. Some regimen, some rule, which he could follow simply, which would take the anxiety out of life. If he had a simple rule of thumb, he thought, he could find relaxation from having followed a simple course of conduct.

The doctor gave him his regimen, a sheet with scheduled

91

things to take and do. But he was pretty certain that his pills and routine would not make the patient strong.

If anxiety is uncontrolled, all the opiates and pills and schedules and regimens won't bring peace and strength. In this patient's case, nothing would bring him good digestion except a shot of cement to stiffen his spine.

Anxiety about whether other people would be offended if he took a stand—well, it remained anxiety as long as he was afraid of their opinions.

What he really needed—what many of us in these hectic times need—is a regimen of the spiritual life. No fretting about surface things, like when to take pill no. 1 or glass of milk no. 3, will help bring peace and strength to the anxious soul.

Jesus gave the man the only course of conduct that would do him any good: "Don't worry and don't keep saying, 'What shall we eat, what shall we drink or what shall we wear?'! That is what pagans are always looking for; your Heavenly Father knows that you need them all. Set your heart on His Kingdom and His goodness, and all these things will come to you as a matter of course."

No rule of thumb will help you if your life is a mess; because it's so easy to live by one rule, only to be all out of control at some other vital point. It takes a principle big enough to cover all of living.

Do you get anxious, all tied in knots? And you want a rule? Well, find out where you have been failing to seek first his Kingdom, where you have been selfish or thoughtless, and remedy that. Then your troubles will vanish.

"Set your heart on His Kingdom and His goodness, and all these things will come to you as a matter of course."

Father, I come to thee, seeking thy truth and goodness, and desiring to be led in thy straight ways. Teach me to walk without fear. AMEN.

your sleep is showing

Maybe you have bags under your eyes? Maybe your skin is as clear and fresh as a daisy, and your eyes sparkle? Your sleep is showing.

LET me tell you of a young man who grew old before his time. He was a man of some position, a man of responsibility in his community. Respected, he was.

People began to note that his face was lined. He looked tired. Then it began to be known that he was away from home a great deal at night, leaving his wife and youngster by themselves. He told them he couldn't sleep, and that he was just going out for a walk.

And when he was away from home, attending conferences, which he did frequently, he could be seen standing on street corners or drinking coffee in a restaurant, until the wee hours.

His eyes grew dull. His face became more heavily lined. People began to wonder about his health. But no one was prepared for the shock when it burst upon them that he had been arrested for a serious crime.

A secret guilt had tortured him for a long time. He had been able to hide it from the waking world, and no one had dreamed what was in his heart.

But his sleep showed. A guilty conscience, a fear that the world would find out what only God and he knew about his depths, had torn him from his bed—denying him that balm of hurt minds, sleep.

After he had been caught and convicted, great as the blow was, great as was the shock to his unsuspecting family, he slept better. He gained weight. His face filled out. Because it was easier to face the world, now that his sleep-disturbing secret was no longer secret.

Your sleep shows. Get enough, refreshing enough, and your eyes, your skin, your bearing, reflect health. Health of the body and of the soul.

We all recognize the look that says, "He is burning the candle at both ends." But sleep is one of those blessings we do not appreciate until we lose them. And when we require too much sleep, and are still unrefreshed in the morning, a bad state of the soul is indicated.

Sleep is a strange thing, which nobody thoroughly understands. But I have a little theory about it. . . . I believe that in sleep the problems we can't work out in our waking time are solved by an unconscious working. Part of the mind continues to function; and some of the great mathematicians have gone to sleep tortured by the effort to find a certain formula, to find that it is ready at hand when they awaken from sleep.

In *Macbeth*, Shakespeare says it this way:

> The innocent sleep,
> Sleep that knits up the ravell'd sleave of care.

The Bible says it this way: "He giveth his beloved sleep" (Psalm 127:2).

Blessings on him that first invented sleep.

Your sleep shows. If in your sleep "little sorrows sit and weep," it should at least show you that you need to straighten out your life. Uneasy lies the head that bears a guilt.

That's why the last five minutes of the day are the most important. Spend the last five minutes before you fall asleep in prayer, asking God for guidance, laying all your faults before him—or just thinking about your heavenly Father and your relation to him—and you can say with David of old, "When I awake, I am still with thee" (Psalm 139:18).

Father, give me that peace of mind, that sweet sleep, that comes from knowing that all is well with my soul. AMEN.

the master was here

> The lives of those to whom Christ is a Friend may be filled with adventure, problem, disappointment, and impatience. . . . But for them life has a purpose. The soul is at peace with God.

THERE is a story, which you may have heard, about the organist of a famous cathedral in the land of Austria. He guarded the instrument carefully. One day a young man came to him and wanted to play the organ. He was denied the privilege by the old organist-guardian, until some argument of the dean of the cathedral persuaded the organist to allow the young stranger to try it.

The young man touched the instrument tenderly. Then he filled the cathedral with the wonder of his music.

The old man said, "Sir, I never knew that my organ could produce such wonderful music. Pray, tell me your name."

The young man replied, "Sir, my name is Felix Mendelssohn."

The old organist was silent for a moment; then he said: "To think . . . that the master musician was here, and I refused to give him the key to my instrument."

To whom do you give the key of your life?

You are a wonderful instrument, responsive to the touch of many forces. And you may give the key to those that play upon your life.

This isn't strange, foreign talk. Don't we talk about giving the keys of our hearts to the ones we love? And "all the world loves a lover." Love plays upon us—and makes us better.

We may open our lives to evil forces. We may be led by weak, conniving people—and then we give off bad, indifferent, or uncertain music.

Does Christ matter? Where does this step of faith, this accepting Christ, lead? The Master is here and calleth for thee.

None of us would dare offer his visible life as something to be copied. None of us would dare say, "Follow the pattern of my life." We know that our imperfections bring discredit to our Lord. Our lives give off an uncertain sound.

Yet there is a common note, common to all who have opened their lives to the Master. There is deep peace within—the peace of God.

That peace is available to you. Christ can offer you an extraordinary joy with it. The lives of those to whom Christ is a Friend may be filled with adventure, problem, disappointment, and impatience; but life has a purpose. Drudgery disappears. The soul is at peace with God.

How you stand in relation to God's claims and Christ's challenge to follow him to newness of life, is the secret of your own mind. If you are conscious of a need for something new and more vital in your life, Christ is the One who can meet that need. The Master is here and calleth for thee.

What are you waiting for? Listen: "Behold, I stand at the door [of your heart], and knock: if any man hear my voice, and open the door, I will come in."

That's all, but that's everything. Let the Master in.

Come into my life, Lord Jesus. Come in today. Show me thy will for my life. AMEN.

what happened to the cow?

*If you are a farmer, you may wonder it
I mean the cow that strayed through a
hole in the fence. If you have just seen
a cow going down the street in a truck,
you may think in terms of hamburgers
and wieners.*

IF I say, "Hey diddle diddle," you know immediately what
happened to the cow. Of course. The cow jumped over the
moon. Do you believe it? . . . Did you see it happen? . . . Have
you proof of it? . . . You don't need proof. You *know* that the
cow in the nursery rhyme jumped over the moon.

Well, now, how much nonsense do you know? Stuff that
you rattle off without a moment's hesitation. You never question
where it came from, what it might mean, how it can be used.
But you know it. Your head is like a closet all neatly filled with
things hanging in just the right places on hooks.

Say, "Hey diddle diddle," and you can reach right in and pick
off, "The cat and the fiddle." Say, "How are you today?" and
you can reach right in and pick off an answer: "Why, I'm fine.
How are you?"—when you may feel wretched and want to
hear how the other guy is about as much as you want to hear
a rehash of the Battle of Waterloo.

But there it is—a mind full of ready nonsense. All right at
hand, because it is repeated so often.

It means nothing. It isn't going to make you a dime. You
don't know where you got it. But there it is.

Would you go on a three-week journey with a bag filled with
toothpicks and paprika and old phonograph needles and hair

nets? You plan to take essentials on a journey, not nonessentials. But how about the journey of life?

Do you have a neat closet filled with essential things in your mind? Suppose up come the words, "I'm distressed." Have you a hook where you may find something right fast to fit the situation? Wouldn't it be nice if you had as ready a response to "I'm distressed" as you have to the cat and the fiddle?

Well, this is the story of a man who filled the holes in his mind (holes opened up there by frustration, loneliness, doubt, and fear) with ready answers. Every morning he propped a page open before him as he shaved, a page filled with wisdom and faith and hope and assurance. And as he shaved, he repeated it to himself, so that the holes in his mind, eaten there by the termites of doubt and despair, were filled.

He now hears: "I'm distressed," and he reaches in and takes out a fitting cloak to take on his journey—"The Lord is thy keeper: the Lord is thy shade upon thy right hand."

He gets a cue: "I'm sad." And he has a ready bit for changing the mood: "I was glad when they said unto me, Let us go into the house of the Lord."

There comes a whispering: "I'm lonely." And, without his having to dig for something in the rubbish in the bottom of his mind's closet, he responds: "Lo, I am with you alway, even unto the end of the world." And his loneliness gives way to:

> What a Friend we have in Jesus,
> All our sins and griefs to bear!

A friend complains: "I'm fearful." And there's a ready answer: "Peace I leave with you, my peace I give unto you."

O Jesus, Master, do thou meet me while I journey in the way, longing to reach a better country, so that by following thee I may keep to the path of faith and righteousness. AMEN.

98

new start

Thus times do shift; each thing his
   turn does hold;
New things succeed, as former things
   grow old.
   —ROBERT HERRICK

where art thou?

The scene of this little story is just outside the east gate of the Garden of Eden. The Lord God is walking in the cool of the evening when he comes upon Adam. Adam is wearing a dark blue suit and a maroon tie. He wears a black Homburg hat and a fancy gold wrist watch.

"WELL, Adam," said the Lord, "it's been a long time since I've seen you around the Garden of Eden. Are you thinking about trying to get back into this place of pleasantness, this delightful garden where there is ease and peace of mind? Where art thou, now?"

"I'm still struggling along, Sir," said Adam, respectfully. "I sweat a different kind of sweat for my daily bread than when I was first set down outside your little paradise. I no longer have to thrive on roots and berries. I've been roasting cattle and freezing vegetables for quite a few years now."

"Yes, I know," answered the Lord God. "I've been watching you. Have you learned anything since you were thrown out for your smart-aleck rebellion?"

"Yes, Sir"—again Adam was quite careful to be reverent. "I've done pretty well at conquering the elements. If I don't tempt fate too far, I can get along with the wind and the storm and the flood O.K. And I've got most of the beasts under control. I am surprised, though, Sir, at the number of beasts. I no sooner get one named than I run across a dozen more. Now I'm exploring the viruses. We get along. Worst trouble I have, though, is still with myself. Eve causes me a little trouble, but mostly I have trouble trying to do the things I know I ought to do."

And the Lord said, "Same old Adam. You were put out of my 'little paradise,' as you call it, because you thought you knew it all. You got just enough of the fruit of good and evil to make you a judge—to judge things that were not your business. I guess you still aren't willing to take my word for what you ought to do."

"Beg pardon, Sir," said Adam. "But this is a new thought to me. I never understood just why you put me out of Eden and made me sweat for my bread. I knew I had rebelled, of course. . . . You say it was because I got a little knowledge, and immediately set myself up as a judge, condemning people?"

"Yes, Adam," said the Lord. "You will notice that I don't judge or condemn my children, but you do. You fuss about the color of their skins, and you think that an unfortunate child ought to be punished instead of loved."

"And you are telling me not to judge?" Adam was lost in thought.

"Thou shalt not judge," said the Lord. . . . "Thou shalt love me first of all, and thy neighbor in the same way. I sent my Son down to show you how to accept my will. He said of his murderers, 'Forgive them; for they know not what they do.' And still you don't learn anything. . . . Your half bite of the knowledge of good and evil makes you want to rival my power, still. Come back in a day or in a thousand years, and show that you've learned to accept my will. Begin where you failed: Learn to accept your brother without judging him. And when you've done these things, we'll talk about your chance to get back into paradise."

Where art thou?

Everything is full of contradiction. I find joy and it turns to sorrow. Until I learn to love thee fully, everything can hurt me. May I learn to love thee so that even my pain and sorrow may be turned to joy and love. AMEN.

this is life

A story without parallel, a swift and sure
drama, the greatest in the world . . .

THIS is a story told by men with microscopes, who can describe the action but who cannot give you the cause.

A cell, no bigger than a pinpoint, meets another cell and absorbs it. The cell divides into two cells. The two cells divide, making four. These divide, and their offspring divide—until by the end of nine months, when the division has repeated itself some forty-five times, there are a thousand billion cells, all working together to be a human life.

Is that you—a thousand billion cells, all of which began as a single cell?

Each of these billions of cells carries on a life of its own. Each appears under the microscope as a lump of jelly, which is constantly changing shape as it absorbs particles from the fluid around it, and digests them. Each chooses some particles by preference. Watch some of these cells when there has been an injury to some portion of the body. They rush to the scene of the injury and there absorb and digest the foreign particles that enter the wound. This scene from the drama of life is a part of the healing process, carried on by individual cells, each living its own independent life.

In the beginning division, all cells are alike. But some in a few short weeks become as hard as the enamel on your teeth, some specialize to form the lens of the eye. Some become red corpuscles carrying iron to trade for oxygen. Each cell specializes into *something* which is helpful to the whole.

From one cell comes a human life. As a dividing mass of cells go to work to form a baby, they form a parasite, living on

103

but not part of, the life of the mother. They are cased in a fluid, in utter darkness.

In that enveloping fluid, in darkness, a drama goes on that stupefies the greatest mind. In the *dark*, where no sight is possible or necessary, certain cells form themselves by a wondrous design into an eye that is *ready* to see. Charles Darwin once said: "I remember well the time when the thought of the eye made me cold all over."

Organs of skin, ear, eye, nose, tongue—all are superfluous in the watery darkness where they are formed. Yet each unhaltingly prepares itself for a daylit, airy world, which it *will* be called upon to report on. One set of cells becomes an outrageously oversized brain, of no use at the moment, but *ready* to learn of the world that is to be experienced. How do they know what is to come?

The full story can't be told in five minutes—nay, in five centuries. But stand in awe before this brief scene of the drama. Before birth the lung is prepared for what *it will do*. But it does not breathe (except as each individual cell is carrying on its independent life). The lung's blood is sidetracked, in the watery darkness, to an artery. At birth this sidetracking of the lung's blood would mean an end to the life. So, in its own time, just at birth, a special muscle closes the channel; and blood flows from the artery to the lung. The lung breathes for all the body! And what of the special muscle, prepared to work just once? It disappears and is never seen again. Exit a hero!

Step by step, as though by some foreknowledge, a single cell has miraculously become a thousand billion cells, each living its own life, but each specialized to work for the whole. This is a human being. This . . . is life.

If you can stand before a fraction of this process and fail to stand in awe at this greatest drama in the world, the Lord pity you.

If you can understand a fraction of the drama within the story, will you join me as we stand in awe before the Maker?

O Lord our Lord, how excellent is thy name in all the earth! . . . What is man, that thou art mindful of him? and the son of man, that thou visitest him? For thou hast made him a little lower than the angels, and hast crowned him with glory and honor. AMEN.

newness of life

A story at least as great as the story of life . . .

HERE is a wealthy man, the owner of vast estates. He has a baby son. Suppose you were to say to him, "Why do you bother about this little child? He is only twenty-two inches long. In size he is nothing, compared with your vast house and grounds and the acres of farm land beyond."

The father would be likely to say in answer, "You have seen my large estates, my house, my treasures. In a sense they are the symbols of my wealth and power. But all I have and am, of which the things you see are only symbols and expressions, are at the disposal of one who is worth more than all of them—though he weighs but eight pounds; for he is my son—he is part of myself."

When we stand in awe at the majesty of God, who has created our universe, and who lovingly fashions the human beings, we must remember that spiritual values are supreme.

Surely he who has fashioned blind matter with such loving and wonderful care, and who takes the trouble to guide the planets in space, will not forget lives that are of infinitely greater value. And he who values a sparrow's fall will not fail those who are of more value than many sparrows. . . . We have the authority of the One who knew God the best.

Surely the true argument is that of the psalmist who put two sentences together, not by accident: "He healeth the broken in heart. . . . He telleth the number of the stars" (Psalm 147:3-4).

We have seen that miraculous changes take place which equip a bundle of cells fashioned in watery darkness for life in an airy world. At birth the baby begins to breathe, is guided by some instinct to know how to eat and how to use an unused stomach. And in many ways this life is marvelously fitted to grow and develop and fit in with a larger plan.

But it is not altogether fitted!

As the baby grows, learning goes on rapidly. The child learns to grasp for what he wants. Other children take his toys. He flies into a rage. As he grows, he must learn to be independent of his mother, who has been his source of life and love for so long. Strange forces move him. He wants to try all experiences. He tries many, looking for happiness, for security.

For a time his chief urge seems to be to grow up, to become independent. He makes enemies. Loved ones desert him. He fears the loss of prestige. People whisper behind his back. He knows that others depend upon him, and his heart burns within him when he fails them. Banks fail, and wars come. He wastes his substance in riotous living.

In short, this life finds difficulty in adjusting with other lives about it. And the inevitable result: it goes astray. All we like sheep have gone astray. Broken in heart, we seek for peace of mind.

One night Nicodemus, a leading Jew and a Pharisee, came to see Jesus. "Master," he began, "we realize that you are a teacher who has come from God. Obviously no one could show the signs that you show unless God were with him."

"Believe me," returned Jesus, "a man cannot even see the Kingdom of God without being born over again."

Here is a miracle as great as that of birth, the miracle of rebirth, by which the one thousand billion cells may again become a part of a greater plan. Spirit gives birth to spirit. That which was born to taste of many experiences, and which has found them bitter, may through the grace of the Son of God find light in the darkness of this world, a true path to the kingdom of God. The true Way may now be known. This is rebirth.

"Seek ye the Lord while he may be found, call ye upon him while he is near."

O Thou who healest the broken in heart and bindest up their wounds, who tellest the number of the stars, heal thou my wounds; give me a new heart. AMEN.

an austere man

About a man who thought a passage of scripture was meant just for him . . .

IN A STREET meeting in Boston the parable of the wicked servant was read—about the nobleman who left ten pounds with his servants. One man took his piece of money and made it multiply ten times for his master. Another said, "Thy pound hath gained five pounds." To reward these men, the Master gave one authority over ten cities, and the other authority over five cities.

The third servant said, "Lord, behold, here is thy pound, which I have kept laid up in a napkin: for I feared thee, because thou art an austere man."

Now an austere man is a hard man.

But it happened that in the crowd was a man from the fish dock, who made oysters his business. And when he heard, "Thou art an austere man," the wheels inside his head began to spin. "I'm an oysterman," he thought.

And he preached a sermon to the assembled men in language they understood. "Life is like an oyster," he said. "The Lord found us in the mud. He cracked our shells. And he found out what we were worth inside."

He heard a passage of scripture. He may not have heard the rest of the preaching, but he thought about the gospel. He applied it to his own experience. He made it his own. And eight persons were converted to Christ as the result of his experience.

Here, in the picturesque words of one man's experience, is the truth of the saving grace of God. "He found us in the mud. He cracked our shells, and found out what we were worth." Doesn't that describe the experience? Everyone who comes to Christ must first realize that he is in the mud—although it may be said in different words. Before you take the steps to finding Christ, you begin by realizing that your life is not right.

And you have built up a shell around yourself. You know that your way of life is wrong, and you don't want anyone to penetrate your shell and see the mess inside. "He cracked our shell, and found out what we were worth." There is the truth. Let the Lord see your secret self, and find that there is a person inside of infinite worth. God loves the person inside that shell so much that he gave his Son to save that person.

I will remember the works of the Lord; surely I will remember thy wonders of old. I will meditate also upon all thy work, and talk of thy doings. AMEN.

sow's ear —
silk purse

What has happened to the old saying, "You can't make a silk purse out of a sow's ear"?

I GUESS this old saying must have been proved false by time; because they've made better than a silk purse out of less promising materials than a sow's ear. They make nylon, which is finer than silk for many things, out of coal.

So the old saying is discredited.

And maybe it's just as well. The old saying used to be applied to human beings. Some worthless fellow appeared to be hopeless, and nobody expected him to change, so they said, "You can't change a leopard's spots," or, "You can't make a silk purse out of a sow's ear."

There are more ancient sayings that will never be discredited by science or by any of man's inventions.

A young preacher returned to the town where he was reared. And he was invited to preach. When he came to the pulpit, he found a penciled note, written by one of his old buddies with whom he had run around before going to seminary. The note listed some of his youthful pranks and escapades.

The young preacher picked up the paper and read it. Quietly he smiled. Then he shared it with the congregation. And he added, "This tells what I used to be, and shows how great is the grace of God, that could save one like me."

Paul wrote to such a young fellow, who was apparently beginning to think of himself as a "sow's ear": "This is a faithful saying, and worthy of all acceptation, that Christ Jesus came into the world to save sinners; of whom I am chief" (I Timothy

1:15). Paul felt that God had singled him out for a "pattern to them which should hereafter believe." He thought of himself as an example of the fact that God can make the best even out of the worst.

We make wonder drugs out of barnyard filth. We make nylon out of coal. But no wonder compares with this: that God can make the best out of the worst of us.

Do you sometimes brood about past failures? Or present weaknesses? Feel like a sow's ear? People around you, able to live freely without your particular problem, able to overcome temptations that look big to you—do they look like silk purses to you? "This is a faithful saying, and worthy of all acceptation, that Christ Jesus came into the world to save sinners."

Paul says that he realized that he was the worst of sinners; and because of this very fact God was particularly merciful to him. It is a demonstration of the extent of God's patience toward the worst of men, to serve as an example to all who in the future should trust in him for eternal life.

Learn to see your failures in this light—as a witness to the transforming power of God—and they will become leads to higher spiritual living.

Dear Lord, help me to love thee more sincerely even through my mistakes. These are lessons thou knowest I must learn. Help me to accept them as right for me. AMEN.